WHAT SHOULD WE TEACH AND
HOW SHOULD WE TEACH IT?

To Bridget Nuttgens who
arranged a mass of material
and made judicious
additions and deletions

What Should We Teach and How Should We Teach It?
Aims and Purpose of Higher Education

Patrick Nuttgens

WILDWOOD HOUSE

Published by
Wildwood House Ltd
Gower House
Croft Road
Aldershot
Hants GU11 3HR
England

and distributed by
Gower Publishing Company
Old Post Road
Brookfield
Vermont 05036
USA

British Library Cataloguing in Publication Data

Nuttgens, Patrick
  What should we teach and
  how should we teach it?
  1. Education—Aims and objectives
  I. Title
  370.11   LB17

Library of Congress Cataloging-in-Publication Data

Nuttgens, Patrick.
  What Should We Teach and How Should We Teach It?

Includes index.
  1. Technical education—Great Britain.   I. Title.
T107.N88   1988   607'.1   87–28189

ISBN 0 7045 3092 9
     0 7045 0578 9 (pbk)

Typeset by Guildford Graphics Limited, Petworth, West Sussex
Printed and bound in Great Britain by
Biddles Limited, Guildford and King's Lynn

Contents

Preface

This book goes to press at a moment in the story of educational change which may prove to be crucial to the future of the country. The government in power for at least the next five years is already involved in decisions about the future pattern of education that may well decide the future prosperity, and certainly the future character, of the nation.

We are at a turning-point. I am convinced that the message and meaning of this book are vital to government policy, for it is concerned with the aims and purpose of education, and with the methods which inevitably help to shape those aims. The issues it raises cannot be ignored.

The writing is the result of some thirty years' work in the teaching and management of higher education, especially the last fifteen years, when I was responsible for putting together and steering a polytechnic. It is therefore a contribution to an urgent debate based upon the hard-won experience of the realities of the situation. And it centres on the two inescapable questions about education at any level and in any place: What should we teach? And how should we teach it? The answers to those questions will dictate the pattern of the future.

Royal Society of Arts
EDUCATION FOR CAPABILITY

There is a serious imbalance in Britain today in the full process which is described by the two words 'education' and 'training'. The idea of the 'educated person' is that of a scholarly individual who has been neither educated nor trained to exercise useful skills; who is able to understand but not to act. Young people in secondary or higher education increasingly specialise, and do so too often in ways which mean that they are taught to practise only the skills of scholarship and science. They acquire knowledge of particular subjects, but are not equipped to use knowledge in ways which are relevant to the world outside the education system.

This imbalance is harmful to individuals, to industry and to society. A well-balanced education should, of course, embrace analysis and the acquisition of knowledge. But it must also include the exercise of creative skills, the competence to undertake and complete tasks and the ability to cope with everyday life; and also doing all these things in co-operation with others.

There exists in its own right a culture which is concerned with doing, making and organising and the creative arts. This culture emphasises the day to day management of affairs, the formulation and solution of problems and the design, manufacture and marketing of goods and services.

Educators should spend more time preparing people in this way for a life outside the education system. The country would benefit significantly in economic terms from what is here described as Education for Capability.

Introduction

In 1965 Anthony Crosland, Secretary of State for Education and Science in Harold Wilson's Labour government, delivered a speech at Woolwich which was to initiate an educational revolution. In it he outlined what came to be known as the binary system – a two-pronged system of higher education which provided for a public sector of higher education alongside the universities. The following year a White Paper set out the creation of the new institutions. They were to be equal in standard to the universities, at least in those areas in which they would offer degrees, but their primary function was to be vocational education. Thirty such institutions were formally designated in the next few years. They were the polytechnics.

The heart of this book is the polytechnic venture – a story which has so far not been written. But I am concerned with more than their story, because the polytechnic experiment must take its place in the history of education in Britain along with comprehensive education, experiments in open learning such as the Open University, and the changes in the examination system which have produced the new leaving examinations common to all children (Standard Grade in Scotland, and GCSE in England and Wales) as part of a new educational experience. It is an experience which has moved away from the liberal tradition of education for education's sake, established in this country now for over 150 years, canonized by Newman in his *Idea of a University*, embodied in Oxford and Cambridge and the foundation of our established examination system as formulated by university-based examination boards. The new experience differs from the established system in its starting-point, its learning processes and its ends. It sees 'hands-on' experience as just as important a source and method of learning as is the scholarly world of books, theories and generalizations; and it aims at education for daily life.

Clearly, such a change in the basic approach and practice of education – indeed, in the very idea of what we mean by education – is revolutionary. To this revolution I have been lucky enough to be able to contribute both on the practical side by setting up the Polytechnic in Leeds and acting as its director for the first fifteen years of its existence; and on the theoretical side, the thinking about education which underlies the changes. Among much writing and lecturing on the subject, one paper of mine in particular, entitled *Learning to Some Purpose*, written for the Burton Award of 1977 and given at the Society of Industrial Artists and Designers, was to play its part in the launching of the movement which later assumed the name of 'Education for Capability'.

This book falls into three parts. First, there is the story – the when and where. This is, of necessity, personal, because experience *is* personal. Parts two and three – the how and why – follow through some of the thinking behind the revolution. This thinking has evolved through a series of writings and lectures – my own and those of like-minded innovators – and through much talking and sharing of experience within the educational world. The book is assembled in that order: first, the practical and particular, leading on to the general and theoretical. The order is important. I am practising what I preach in the succeeding pages, and from the start orienting the reader to approach education from a new direction. For one of my basic conclusions is that the conventional form of our education, exam-oriented as it is, which presents the student first with the theory and then moves on to practical application if time allows, is in fact the inverse of the natural psychology of the learning process. In real life we experience something, and from that experience acquire a vocabulary to assimilate the experience (find the words that make it possible to reflect on it), and only then are capable of formulating a concept, the theory. Observation of a small child learning about life makes this obvious.

As it happens, I have myself moved from the conventional tradition of education to the new one, and so my personal story makes a suitable introduction to the new thinking. In 1962 I came south from Edinburgh University, where I had held a lectureship in architecture, to run the Institute of Advanced Architectural Studies, one of the two graduate institutions incorporated into the new University of York. The Institute ran short courses for professional architects, and therefore I had no undergraduate students – a position which made some of my colleagues envious. They saw my position as similar to that highly coveted position among academics – being a fellow of All Souls, Oxford – particularly since the Institute was housed first in an old church and then in one of the historic buildings owned by the University, the mainly sixteenth and seventeenth-century King's Manor in the heart of the city. Parts of the Manor were older than that and had been the abbot's house for St Mary's Abbey whose ruins are today used as a backdrop for the Mystery Plays during the York Festivals. My own office was in a medieval room which had been the abbot's kitchen.

When I left in 1969, I held a personal professorship at

York. I moved to the more commercial and industrial city of Leeds to unite a collection of disparate and under-funded colleges of further education, centred on an ugly concrete 'egg-crate' in the city centre, and create from them a polytechnic. Geographically, York and Leeds are only 26 miles apart. Aesthetically, the two institutions could have been in different worlds, and the distance on the social scale in terms of status was immense.

Why did I move? Many colleagues and friends simply thought I had gone mad. Some saw even more sinister implications – I was fleeing from debts or extramarital entanglements, or had been privily eased out because of a drink problem. Others presumed I'd sold my soul to mammon: 'It's the money – must be.' Since I am notoriously vague about what I am earning, I can only confirm that it wasn't the money! I hope some answer to the question will be given by this book, as I chart some of the new routes through education that those of us in the forefront of the new movement have plotted. I would like to think that as a result of our efforts, British education will never be the same again. For we are at the end of the era to which conventional education belongs. Human nature may not have changed fundamentally but the world for which we are educating and training our young, and sometimes older, people has changed dramatically in the 150 years since that education effectively took on its present shape. We also live in a pragmatic world, characterized by changes unforeseen by the majority but affecting them fundamentally, in which the belief in abstract truths, however fundamental, may be less important than an understanding of what is happening in the world.

Consider these facts. It is just over 100 years since Forster's Education Act of 1870 brought elementary education within the reach of all children. There are now more than ten million children and young people in full-time attendance at schools, universities, polytechnics, colleges of education and further education. Their increase reflects other major changes in society.

In 1832 the electorate of the United Kingdom was 500,000 — that is, a vote for about one person in 50. As a result of the Reform Act in that year and subsequent Acts the proportion changed dramatically: by the 1880s more than one adult in six had a vote. In this century the enfranchisement of women over 30 gave the vote to nearly half the population. The 1969 Act, in which 18 year olds were given the vote, meant that the electorate was 40 million out of a population of roughly 54 million.

Sources of information have dramatically increased. Before the turn of the century a major newspaper, *The Daily Telegraph*, had a circulation of about 300,000. Now we regard as common among the major dailies a printing of four million or more and a readership many times that. In the last 40 years the development of radio and television means that the number of people reached by these media includes virtually all the population. It is thought that most people watch television for at least 21 hours a week, which means that by the time a student arrives at university or college he or she has probably spent two or three years of waking life watching the box; and by retirement will have spent 12 years of waking life watching it.

These changes — in general education, in social responsibility, in the availability of information — must mean that the total intellectual and social scene has been transformed. In the education world, it is not just the case that more opportunities are available; it is the case that new kinds of subject are studied, that new kinds of qualifications are available, that traditional kinds of qualification, such as degrees, have been reinterpreted to include areas of activity never previously considered appropriate. The relationship between the individual and society, between the branches of the media, between one educational establishment and another, have been fundamentally altered.

Such considerations point up the necessity for rethinking the educational system. So this book is an exploration, an attempt to find out what is seriously amiss and what radical rethinking must be done if we are to correct a serious imbalance in our educational system. I am not alone in considering the problem. A growing number of people – academics, industrialists, business people, politicians – are asking fundamental questions about our educational system and its underlying assumptions. Other countries have different traditions. We had always taken it for granted in this country that we had got it right. Faced by the evidence of the gulf between the world of educational institutions and the world of work for which our students are ostensibly being prepared, many of us are not so confident. Increasingly, we are finding the courage to ask if we have perhaps got it wrong. And we also ask if there is a more positive and creative way of looking at our educational inheritance and our educational future. It may be vital for the prosperity and success of the country. But more than that: it may be crucial for the happiness and satisfaction of the people to find ways of living and behaving which recognize the fantastic possibilities of life in an age revolutionized by high technology and revealed by the wonders of communications.

That involves education for all; and it involves all parts of education. It is central to the argument of this book that the educational experience has to be seen as a whole. For it is the whole that requires scrutiny, not just a few parts. The book therefore looks at education at all levels, and after an analysis of its present problems, tries to set out the grounds for a more appropriate philosophy of education, and work its way towards the studies and activities that might be developed in and after school. But the starting-point of the argument is higher education, and this is not only (or even chiefly) because this is my own area of expertise, but for a reason which is fundamental to the contemporary situation — namely, that all education in this country is influenced by higher education and ultimately by the universities. That is a contention which I shall develop at length at its due place in my argument.

Since I started working on this book, there are signs that the basic principles of 'Education for Capability', as enuntiated in the manifesto printed at the start of this book, are emerging from the realm of ideas and assuming practical shape in new forms of work/education partnerships and transitions. We stand at the entry to a new educational era.

PART 1
IN SEARCH OF REALITY:
A PERSONAL STORY

1 Towards the Polytechnic

It was only when I embarked on my personal story that I realized to what an extent the two traditions of education which I am shortly to examine — education for its own sake (based on intellectual theories) and education for some purpose (where learning is acquired by practical experience) — have been present throughout my life.

My mother, who died when I was seven, was by all accounts an intellectual — a red-haired, strong-minded, strong-willed Irish woman with a prodigious memory, who had studied mathematics under De Valera, and became involved in the political controversy shaking Ireland in the 1920s. After an incident when drunken Black-and-Tans raided the family farmhouse with drawn pistols and searched it for arms, my grandfather, who was a local JP, declared he would court no further such excitements and sent my mother to England out of harm's way. She became a governess in Chipping Campden in the Cotswolds, where she met my father, who was working there in a stained-glass studio.

Chipping Campden is a name long associated with the Arts and Crafts tradition. No industrial concerns were set up in the little town during the nineteenth century to disturb its memories of a pre-industrial eighteenth-century cottage craft tradition. So it must have seemed a suitable place for Charles Robert Ashbee at the turn of the century to move to with his Guild of Handicraft from the Mile End Road of London's East End, when he was seeking a more rural setting for his community of 150 people. Ashbee was a silversmith, jewellery designer and architect and a devotee of the Arts and Crafts Movement who sought to translate the theories of John Ruskin and William Morris into a practical reality in keeping with the twentieth century. In *Craftsmanship in Competitive Industry* (1908) he expressed the intention of showing that

> this Arts and Crafts Movement, which began with the earnestness of the Pre-Raphaelite painters, the prophetic enthusiasm of Ruskin and the titanic energy of Morris, is not what the public have thought it to be: a nursery for luxuries . . . for the rich. It is a movement for the stamping out of such things by sound production on one hand and inevitable regulation of machine production and cheap labour on the other . . . The men of this movement . . . want to put in the place of the old order which is passing away, something finer, nobler, saner; they want to determine the limitations of the factory system, to regulate machinery, to get back to realities in labour and human life. (*Craftsmanship in Competitive Industry*, Essex House, Campden, Glos., 1904, p.10)

Ashbee's venture lasted from 1902 to 1907 when the Guild had to be wound up due to its remoteness from the market for handcrafted goods.

My father did not come to Chipping Campden until some years later, in the 1920s, but the spirit of Ashbee's Guild still lived on in the little town, in other craftsmen such as the stained-glass artist, Paul Woodroffe, for whom my father worked. That spirit was to have an important influence on my father's thinking and life, and so, inevitably, on the atmosphere in which I grew up. This conviction that the true artist is his own craftsman, not the superior intellectual who designs the concept but leaves the actual carrying out to a lowly artisan, was further impressed on my upbringing after my father set up on his own as a stained-glass artist in Buckinghamshire. Here, when I was about three, he settled in a village at the bottom of a hill, at the top of which the sculptor, writer and designer of typefaces, Eric Gill, had set up what was to be his last community of artists. Both my parents were what is called 'cradle' Catholics; Gill was a convert to Catholicism, so a further strand was added to the atmosphere of discussion and arguing that permeated my childhood: not only art and design, and the central position of work in life that developed from William Morris's socialist theories, but a dimension concerned with how Man's aspirations and creative activity in life accorded with matters infinite and eternal. Eric Gill's studio was a hive of activity and a talking-shop; many avantgarde thinkers came and went on Pigotts Hill. My father was at one stage local chairman to the Distributists' League. I am told that as a child I sat on the knee of the founder of Distributism, G.K. Chesterton, at a party at his house in Beaconsfield, though looking at photographs of G.K.C.'s bulk, I imagine it was more a case of perching than sitting.

All these things must have bred in me a respect for the culture of doing and making quite as great as my respect for things academic. But undoubtedly the greatest formative influence on me was my father himself, a man who had many of the qualities of a Renaissance universal man — but without the bombast. His father was a tailor's cutter from Aachen with *wanderlust*. He worked in Rome, Paris, Brussels and London where he fell in love with the city and a girl from Norfolk, and settled in Marylebone. My father left school at fourteen in the year George V came to the throne, and

I often wonder if this most cultivated of men was a freak or a typical product of an elementary education in Victorian and Edwardian times. If the latter, there may be lessons here for the educators of today. What is certain is that my father was not only an excellent artist but had as lively a mind as I have encountered, and was outstandingly articulate on paper. He was inexhaustibly knowledgeable about art, architecture and music; he read widely – theology, history, criticism – and was an inveterate letter-writer. By the time of his death at the age of 90 he had, after 70 years of working in glass, became the person in Britain who knew most about the craft of stained-glass-making. As children we were often subjected to readings from Cobbett or Piers Ploughman or Chesterton at mealtimes, and it was a regular thing to be woken by the sound of Mozart's sonatas played very fast, or else Beethoven or Purcell (those were his favourites) on the studio piano. He left no list of his work, but I estimate he must have made over 300 windows, and had demonstrated his craft in a couple of television films – one programme in a series called *In the Making* (BBC2, 1977) which showed particular craftsmen at their craft, and (to demonstrate a craftsman still working in the skills and traditions of the Arts and Crafts Movement) in a sequence in a programme about the turn of the century that I made in a BBC series on English architecture called *The Spirit of the Age*.

This rough sketch of my home background may lay a trail of clues to my attitude to education in later years. My schooling was perhaps more orthodox: I was sent away to Ratcliffe College, a Catholic public school run by the Institute of Charity (the Rosminian fathers) in Leicestershire, where I was taught by some excellent teachers who, I noted even at the time, were not necessarily those with the highest academic qualifications. But even in this phase of my life I did not stick rigidly to the beaten track. At the age of twelve I contracted polio and spent 18 months in a hospital for spinal diseases run by the Sisters of Charity (the nuns with the big white, sail-like hats) in Pinner, Middlesex. Because the majority of patients there were tubercular cases, the wards opened on the outer elements at the front, and we would lie on our beds looking out over the valley towards London, sometimes watching snow fall, sometimes flying bombs (for this was during the war). Other elements of my education at this period included learning to talk Cockney rhyming slang and to speak with a Cockney accent, reading the entire works of Agatha Christie, and organizing and running a Scout troop from my bed.

It could be said that none of this was preparation for an orthodox transition from school to higher education. And so it turned out. My experience of higher education was definitely affected by a decision that I took at school against the advice of my teachers. When, in the sixth form, it was already clear that I would obtain some good results, it was assumed that I would proceed to the University of Cambridge, there to study History or English. In fact, by the time I was 16 or 17 I had decided that I wanted to study architecture, partly because I wished to be some kind of an artist, partly because I had a lasting fascination for old buildings – cathedrals, churches and village buildings of the vernacular kind with which I had become familiar throughout my childhood.

It happened at the time that the School of Architecture at the University of Cambridge could only take students up to the intermediate level of the professional examinations, and thereafter they had to go on to another college to complete their studies, as well as obtain some practical experience in an architect's office before qualifying.

Despite advice, even advice from a Cambridge don who was sent for to steer me in the right direction, I decided not to go to Cambridge but to apply to the College of Art in Edinburgh, whose School of Architecture had a good

16

reputation. Most people thought I was out of my mind to reject the possibility of a place at Cambridge, and I must say that when I saw Cambridge some two or three years later, I thought that I must have been out of my mind myself.

In fact, life and study in a college of art is probably more interesting and certainly more sociable and community-forming than anything I later experienced in a university. Edinburgh was a stunningly beautiful, gaunt, grim and evocative city, and the College of Art had the strength and toughness which went with the city and also with the accident of being a member of that golden generation after the Second World War. I was, I think, among my colleagues in the studio the only one who had not been in the services. That was itself an education.

On the other hand, the first year of architectural studies was boring and superficial compared to the studies I had undertaken in the sixth form at my school. That is not an unfamiliar situation; it happens in universities as well. The level to which one takes one's studies before leaving school is probably higher than anything that happens for at least the first half of the first year at college.

There were enormous compensations — taking out classes in the evening in antique and life drawing, spending many afternoons walking round the closes and wynds and streets of Edinburgh, constantly sketching, thinking and talking about old buildings and new ones. But what effectively changed my life in the College of Art in Edinburgh was the foundation of a degree in architecture, promoted jointly by the College of Art and the University of Edinburgh. It was, I suppose, the most ill-founded course of academic study ever devised. On the other hand, it was very fascinating.

The position was broadly this. The architectural profession being anxious to have university graduates among its members, the School of Architecture in the College of Art made arrangements with the University to enable its students — or at least those of its students who had university entrance qualifications — to take out other subjects in the University in order to qualify for the degree of Master of Arts in the University. Subjecting the entire architectural curriculum to the requirements of the University's MA Honours programme, it was decided that students who took the course would do the whole of their architectural studies at the College of Art and in addition would take out a series of university subjects. I took English, History of Art, Moral Philosophy and an Honours course in Aesthetics, in successive years, and rounded it all off with a written thesis.

The problem was that I had to carry out all the architectural programmes as well. No concessions were made. I was the first student, and in the end, after five people had struggled through the course, it was wound up and replaced by a degree specifically in architecture. I tried it out partly because I had good entrance qualifications, but more because of the persuasion of a fellow student who wanted a companion but failed rather disastrously after a brief but colourful career.

There were certain special problems. The first professor, who arrived from London to be both professor in the University and Head of the School of Architecture at the College of Art, was a most fascinating, exotic and totally irresponsible man who, it was said, had opened a lot of bank accounts with overdrafts all on the strength of one university salary. After a spendid year and a half in the College of Art, during which I was his only university student and a great admirer of his style and panache, he was persuaded to seek his future in the University of Hong Kong, where he had a career as spectacular and disastrous as he had had in Edinburgh. From Hong Kong he went to Salt Lake City, and from there back to London where, alas, he died.

The problem for me was not the professor, but the absence

of a professor. When he left after a year and a half, I found myself taking a course for which no one was in charge and few had any sympathy. It was clearly essential to understand the course myself. It was said at that time that anyone who could understand the Calendar or Prospectus of the University of Edinburgh deserved an Honours degree; I became convinced that I deserved one just for understanding what had happened. I directed my own studies, with one almost disastrous exception at the end, but generally with efficiency and calm.

In characteristic university style, my director of studies was a lecturer in the Department of Medieval History, a most brilliant and likeable man who knew nothing about my course. I went to see him at the beginning of October each year. He groaned audibly as I came into his room, would hold his head and say, 'Oh dear, Nuttgens. Are you prepared to swear that what you have put on this piece of paper which I am about to sign is exactly right and represents what you should be doing this year?' I would cross my hands over my heart and swear that it was right. He then signed the paper after saying, 'I will sign on one condition — that under no circumstances will you come back to see me for at least a year.'

With that happy introduction I got on with the course and learned a basic lesson about life in the universities or in the colleges, or indeed anywhere else — that there is nothing to replace being responsible for yourself. Perhaps that is what all universities ultimately teach.

It became clear to me that there were marked contrasts between the College of Art, the University, and the local Technical College (now the Heriot-Watt University) to which we went two or three afternoons a week to learn structural engineering, being taught by ancient lecturers who had been allocated to the ignorant architects and whose interest in their activity was marginal. The College of Art was friendly, small, immediate, vital, fairly anti-intellectual, but fun. The University was daunting. It was enormous; it seemed unfriendly and quite uninterested in its students. On the other hand, it was intellectually one of the most stimulating periods of my life. Not just in the lectures, most of which were given in an incompetent and desultory way, but in terms of the social and intellectual life built up by the students themselves in debating societies, dramatic and literary and other societies – many of which I belonged to. The Technical College, in still further contrast, appeared to me without character or life of any kind.

In the middle of this eccentric course, and partly to recover from three years of overwork, I transferred for a year to the School of Drawing and Painting while taking my Honours course in Aesthetics. That was again tremendous fun. I did enough painting to convince myself that I was never going to be a great painter and that it was time to return to the School of Architecture.

It solved for the time being a problem which affects anybody studying different disciplines. As the years went on I realized that the most difficult, tiresome and time-consuming factor in the whole of this bizarre course of instruction was transferring from one subject to another. To go out of the studio, walk along the road, go to a lecture in English, transfer one's attention to a book on philosophy, and then come back to a class in structural engineering or drains – all of this was immensely taxing to the mind and convinced me that most people's minds, including my own, were not nearly as flexible as one would like.

I came out of this experience with a reasonable general record, a medal in English and a first class Honours degree in Architecture, having written a long thesis on the architecture of the Black Friars in England and Scotland. What I did not come out with was a really good record in architectural design, which was what I had set out to do. It was therefore not altogether surprising to me when the new professor who arrived when I was in my last year at college offered me a grant so that I could undertake research into a subject that interested him — the vernacular architecture of Scotland. I spent a happy two years studying ordinary buildings — cottages, farm buildings, mills and bridges — in the north-east Lowlands of Scotland. I was attached to the School of Scottish Studies, a research institute in the University of Edinburgh.

There were many new experiences and lessons for me as I carried out that work. I became convinced that research by itself without teaching was destructive of the human personality. It may have been accidental that the School of Scottish Studies was at the time riddled with the most vicious internal rivalries. Some researchers seemed to spend all their time writing memoranda, organizing round-robins, spreading fantastic rumours about the behaviour of their fellows. As a junior person attached temporarily to it, I watched this with admiration and despair.

I found, as before, that I had to supervise my own work. I believe it is a general experience that students taking a PhD (it had earlier been decided that the best way to focus my studies was to aim for a Doctorate in Philosophy) get very little supervision, partly because of the absence of their supervisors, more likely because within a year or possibly even a term, the researcher is already better informed than the supervisor. That was one aspect. A more significant one was that I was undertaking research which involved a number of different disciplines. It became necessary to study subjects which I had not formerly done and therefore to study them at a level which was fairly elementary even though I was myself engaged in postgraduate work. Postgraduate work, in other words, is not all of one level. In this case I had to use the library and read up geography and physics, neither of which subjects I had taken at school or university. Partly because of that, and also because of my interest in architectural books and in general literature, I became very familiar with the Library of the University of Edinburgh, which in those days was housed in the Old College. Rumour had it that students had disappeared into the furthest depths of the Library and never been seen again. Some of the books I wanted were lodged in attics in which mysterious people were to be found from time to time, sallow, drawn and deranged, presumably still making notes years after their disappearance from the ordinary world.

My research however also took me round the country, living for a year in a fisherman's house on the edge of the Moray Firth, driving in a battered, second-hand car, talking to the owners of farms and cottages and mills, taking photographs whenever I could, working in estate offices and tracing plans and drawings of farm buildings, until I had built up a fairly large archive of material mostly of the eighteenth and nineteenth centuries. That was also itself an education.

Long before I had finished the doctorate, however, a major change had taken place in the teaching of architecture in Edinburgh, when the professor left the College of Art and was entrusted by the University with the setting-up of a separate department in the University. Being to some extent on the spot, I was given a part-time lecturer's job with a view to helping the professor in the setting-up of the new course. This meant trying to understand and work on the ordinances and regulations for the new degree of Bachelor of Architecture, as well as beginning to plan the actual course.

Looking back on it now, I am almost jealous of the freedom I had to plan a course *de novo*. Such a privilege was not unfortunately obvious to the person engaged in the work at the time. It requires considerable maturity. At the time I was frightened of the fact that there appeared no guidelines, no rules, nothing to tell us what we ought to be doing. And since I myself was singularly short of practical experience in architecture, I found myself thrown back on talking, reading, constantly picking people's brains, hoping all the time to find a rationale or the basis for a course.

It was clear to me from the start that architecture in the University was not among the reputable subjects that a university usually taught. Rumour had it that the Professor of English had remarked at the Senate that if the University were going to teach architecture, it would be teaching plumbing next. In fact, as the Professor of Architecture later remarked, it does now teach plumbing, but calls it Building Science.

It occurred to me, being one of the few university graduates in architecture in Scotland, and having been fascinated by my studies in English and in philosophy, that I might turn my mind to proving how conventional as an academic discipline architecture was. I therefore carried out a study of architectural education, and, after many discussions and arguments, produced my own analysis of architecture in terms of academic categories. Architecture depended, I thought, on four basic disciplines – the disciplines of Science, Philosophy, Art and Design. Design was what we specifically had to offer. All the other disciplines were disciplines studied better and to a higher level in other departments. Design was something of our own. It was essential, it seemed to me, to insist that Design was an activity every bit as formidable and as fundamental as the discipline of Science. The problem was, of course, to know exactly what Design was. It was an even greater problem in university terms to say how Design could function like a university discipline, the main characteristics of which were criticism and understanding and in principle the pursuit of the subject no matter where it might lead. Our offering – Design – was essentially creative.

It often depended upon inadequate information, required all sorts of snap judgements, and had to be completed in order to exist at all. It consumed very long hours, it might not be very verbal, and our best students might not be particularly articulate. Nevertheless, I decided that academic disciplines were the very essence of university study and research.

Because of the nature of architecture there was always a tension between academic learning and practical experience. I myself was short of experience; some of my colleagues had plenty of it, but were short of academic expertise. Hoping to bring the whole thing together, the professor obtained some money from a foundation and set up a research project into housing. That, once again, led to fantastic disruption inside the department, which affected my attitude towards the department and, I suppose, towards research. Even while the department was small it became clear to me that there was a constant tension between the activity of teaching and the need to do research. My own fascination was with teaching.

Taking off a summer I completed the thesis and obtained a PhD. But the exciting part of the work was teaching students, particularly senior students, not only teaching them architectural design but engaging in seminars and discussions, with people from other disciplines, trying between us to discover an education which would stand us all in good stead no matter what in the end we might do. I stood somewhere on a threshold between the activities of making, designing, drawing, thinking and creating, and the disciplines of philosophy, history and science.

It was mainly because of my wish to extricate myself from the difficulties and bad feeling of the research project that I attended a Summer School in York on historic buildings and in due course was recruited as one of the first members of the new University, to take over the existing Institute of Advanced Architectural Studies and become a Reader in the University.

When I arrived in York the University consisted of the Vice-Chancellor, Lord James, the Registrar, some administrative staff and myself. About five or six other academics had been appointed but were not due to take up their appointments for another six months. What intervened was a series of Lord James's 'long weekends' when we would gather on a Friday, stay till the Sunday afternoon or evening, have long discussions organized and led by him on the nature of the University, what it might do, what would be some of its problems, how it should be structured and how we might work out the implications of the general comments made by the advisory committee on the setting-up of the University.

It was an extraordinarily exciting experience. I commuted for quite a long time between Edinburgh and York, took over the Institute, and played a junior but active part in the discussions about the University itself. It was obvious from the start that there were at least two different concepts of a university among us. The Vice-Chancellor, Lord James, unmistakeably had an idea. It was, I suppose, a Platonic idea. He was a devotee of Plato, who was used on many occasions either to back up arguments or to raise questions as we continued our discussions – which were largely on the nature of a university. It seemed to follow that we would constantly refer to Newman's *Idea of a University* – at that time one of the few fundamental texts we could use to discuss the nature of learning and the nature of higher education. As far as I remember we did not refer to Whitehead's *Aims of Education and Other Essays*.

I became aware of a fascinating polarity. The Vice-Chancellor's ideas were based upon his experience as a student at Oxford, and then of teaching, with great brilliance, in very good schools — first Winchester and then Manchester Grammar School, of which he had been the High Master. He saw the University as a social/academic unity pursuing excellence, sufficient unto itself, independent and autonomous. Its social life was essential to its academic studies; hence the concept of colleges, to one of which every member of staff as well as every student would belong. On the other hand, the only academic recruited at the start who was already a professor was Alan Peacock, who had been Professor of Political Economy in the University of Edinburgh and since probably best known for the Peacock Report on the BBC's finances. He was a more single-minded specialist. Where James was concerned with the unity of the whole, Peacock was concerned with the excellence of its component parts, in his case the Department of Economics. Enough excellent parts would add up to an excellent university.

I have forgotten much of the discussions that took place. What sticks in my mind were the pragmatic things: for example, the discussion about the nature of departments. There was no question of the type of departments we would set up: they would be departments based upon subjects, or disciplines. They were therefore English, History, Mathematics, Philosophy, Economics, Politics, Sociology, Physics, Chemistry, Biology. It had been decided as well that there would be a Department of Music. That introduced a rather different activity, which was more like Architecture.

One of the inherent weaknesses in the plan was revealed by the problem of servicing between departments. James believed that service teaching by people from one discipline, of students taking another, was almost always unsuccessful. He was right. But the problem is fundamental and inescapable given the normal academic structure of a university. If it is organized by subjects, and if the subjects have the money to handle the promotions, the subjects will be in control and genuine collaboration between them be minimal. But nearly all serious development nowadays involves more than one subject and is interdisciplinary.

A more direct effect was the work and attitudes of the architects for the site and the new buildings. Whatever happens in the case of existing institutions, it must be the case that in the beginning of a university, especially a brand new university on a green site, the decisions of the development planners, the architects, are crucial to what can happen. Although the academics always denied this, I felt sure that the architects for the development had a profound effect upon academic development.

It so happened that the architects for the University of York had a background in the Ministry of Education, where in the post-war years they had developed not only systems of prefabrication, but a way of approaching the design of buildings based upon as precise as possible a performance specification. In this they were unlike most of the academics, even though those who join a new university are more of buccaneers than typical academics. In the academic mind there is a great advantage in indecision. It enables one to retain a reputation for calmness, judgement and independence. It is at the moment when one has actually to do something and make a decision about a place or a thing, that one's reputation for impartiality is destroyed.

Some important decisions about the University of York were, I believe, fostered by the architects, however much in consultation. For example, it was decided early on that the departments would be separate little buildings reached from the walkways between colleges, never big enough to house all the staff in that particular subject; the rest would be dispersed among the colleges. After a long discussion it was decided to put all the departments into colleges; but they did not follow any logical order and they would never be complete. The exception to this was Economics; to meet the professor's demands a special building had to be put up for Economics as well as the adaptation of an older building for its Research Unit.

Looking back on it now, there is an interesting contrast in success and failure. James's basic plan was, I believe, an overall success. The colleges are still, in his phrase, a tender plant, but they had a reality and an identity from the start, which has created an atmosphere and a sense of community which made York remarkably free of student trouble of any serious kind at the end of the 1960s.

On the other hand, the isolates in Economics were one of the few groups that had a serious sit-in which prevented their working. Furthermore, the initial grouping together of the Social Sciences − Economics, Politics and Sociology − as a unity was illusory. And that was for me an important recognition. In a complex university the components are not really the simple ones that feature in a plan. We might group ourselves into faculties, which is broadly what they had tried to do. But faculties are more artificial than the whole university. The realities, if one is going to teach by subjects, are the subjects. If, therefore, one wanted to make a different kind of structure and to encourage the interdisciplinary nature of learning and study, it was essential to found the departments in a different way.

Meantime, what was happening to architecture? The Institute of Advanced Architectural Studies was one of the two original institutes which led to the formation of the University. Like the Borthwick Institute of Historical Research, it had been founded during the interim when the government, with characteristic perception, had announced that there was no case for the foundation of any new universities. In the 1950s, therefore, the Architectural Institute was built up by the York Academic Trust to run courses, originally on the restoration of old buildings, then in an increasing variety of topics. All the courses were professional; they were technical; they were specific; they were short courses attended by architects and planners, builders and engineers, and many other professionals associated with the building of the environment. Some of the most interesting had to do with economics in central area planning; some of the most exciting dealt with professional collaboration, that is, designing a building with all the different professionals involved according to a plan and a programme.

It quickly became clear to me that mid-career people coming on a course could not be fobbed off with generalities of a normal educational kind. For example, it was clear that the lecturers and organizers of seminars and discussions on the courses had in the main to be people from practice. The number of professional teachers we used was almost nil. The subject-matter needed to be immediate and practical.

The fact is that both in the planning of courses, in the subject-matter, and in the way in which they are run, mature people are in search of reality. And that for most people trying to earn a living means a reality that has to do directly with their mode of life and with the extension of its possibilities. The call for quality had to be a part of the urge for efficiency and competence and satisfaction in the ordinary round of daily work. It followed from this that the Architectural Institute occupied a somewhat eccentric place in the University of York. I could not avoid the conclusion that had the University of York been founded first it would not have found it necessary to develop an Institute of Advanced Architectural Studies. And yet architecture was central to the City of York. It was not only the courses on the restoration of buildings, on the management of projects, on the problem of organizing the reassembly and redevelopment of old areas; it was also that the City of York itself offered very real problems that had to be solved. For example, there was the minster whose restoration was undertaken by Bernard Feilden — one of the earliest and most regular attenders on courses at the Institute; there was the whole problem of town planning in York and the conservation of buildings which became a crisis in the mid-1960s and in which I played a part in provoking the arguments and discussion which led ultimately to a changed policy.

While the University as a whole kept its distance from the city and occupied itself on the site at Heslington, described by the Vice-Chancellor as an off-shore island, the members of the Architectural Institute engaged in all sorts of activities and controversies to do with the change of the actual environment in which we were living and working. As we did so, it became clear to me that it was crucial in any academic community that it should be involved with the community as a whole; and that the community as a whole should be involved with it.

York is not the same as it was when the University was founded. It is certainly more self-conscious, probably more self-critical. The sections of the University which played the greatest part in the life of the city were architecture, music (which plays an important part in the York Festival) and history. History is interesting because, from the start, probably because of the influence of the Borthwick Institute and its archives, it drew upon York and its region as a rich mine of historical material. With that experience it seemed to me that the links with the city depended upon the use and exploitation of local material and the development of action in music, in the arts, and in design. It seemed logical that the University should develop, outside term-time, as a successful centre for conferences, courses and meetings. It was in fact in danger of becoming a better conference centre than a university.

To make a move from the University of York to the new polytechnic in Leeds was to go through an experience which was deeply traumatic. Before I left York, I had become a professor in the University; and not only a professor, but a professor without undergraduate students — a state regarded by most academics as arcadian. Until I ceased to be a professor I had not realized what status was accorded to a professor by the country as a whole. Why did I leave? The immediate reason was the inability of the University — not its own fault, but simply through lack of money — to found the undergraduate architectural school which I had been hoping to start. That happened at the same time as a crisis affected the School of Architecture in Leeds College of Art, which it had been proposed for many years to transfer to the University, and which was now prevented by lack of money as well. In the course of chairing a joint committee of the University of Leeds and the Leeds Education Authority to sort out the future of the School of Architecture, the Polytechnic was designated; I applied for the post and moved to the Polytechnic as its first Director. And there was a more positive side to it. Reversing T.S. Eliot's dictum that humankind cannot bear too much reality, I used to explain to my friends that my kind could only bear so much paradise on earth. I was anxious to deal with students, to be involved in teaching rather than research. I wanted a challenge.

2 The Polytechnic

And it proved a challenge. My ignorance of the educati al
system, both national and local, was profound. Until I moved
to Leeds, I had no idea how confused, overlapping, irrational
and ill-assorted was the organization of education in this
country. The polytechnics occupied in any case an odd position
between local and national government. They were owned
by the local authority but they had a task which was national
in its scope. All the administrative parties were able to frustrate
things; few of them were able to behave with any real authority.
In the case of the local authority there was a fundamental
problem which I had not appreciated before arriving but very
shortly thereafter did, which was its decision to keep a firm
control over the Polytechnic by putting the approval of its
work under at least two separate committees of the Council
– the academic side under Education and the non-academic
staff (administrative, secretarial and technical) under Establishment. This was calculated to create the utmost confusion and
a grotesque imbalance in the planning of the personnel functions
of the Polytechnic. But that, I began to appreciate was reality.
It was the harsh reality, not just of inadequate financial provision, but of the confusion of motives, between lots of different
kinds of people.

That is in a way characteristic of the Polytechnic world
– its plurality. The Polytechnic contained lots of different kinds

of people. It was formed by the amalgamation of four colleges
– the College of Commerce, the College of Technology,
the College of Art and the Yorkshire College of Education
and Home Economics (a teacher training college). The people
from them were very different in character and in their
attitudes. Commerce was based on courses; the staff had
considerable involvement in private practice and in looking
after their own affairs. Technology was mainly based upon
disciplines as departments, but was riddled with an inferiority
complex caused largely by the proximity of the University
of Leeds with its big departments of Civil, Electrical and
Mechanical Engineering. Art had a great reputation, mainly
created by a man who was no longer there, Harry Thubron;
it was highly original, fairly avantgarde, extraordinarily well
financed and rather smug. The teacher training college
contained an efficient section in Institutional Management,
but as far as teacher training was concerned had lower
standards of entry than any other part of the Polytechnic.
It is interesting that the two constituent colleges which were
considered outstanding nationally were *not* technological: they
were Art, and the Carnegie College of Physical Education
which was to join the Polytechnic with the teacher training
colleges some years later.

I found that it was necessary to declare my attitude to
this new polytechnic right at the start when, during my
interview for the post of Director, I was asked if I felt I
had sufficient experience to tackle the administration of a
large-scale institution. I pointed out that they were shortly
to appoint a Chief Administrative Officer, and that I did
not see my job as that of an administrator. I felt that my
role was to be the leader of the institution both academically
and in policy-making. The division of the Polytechnic management that I eventually evolved was that I should be supported
by three Assistant Directors, each with a particular responsi-

bility for one area — academic, resources and personnel. It is possible that in this division of the work I was influenced by my own experience in the setting up of York University with its officers. But in the organization of the academic or teaching areas of the Polytechnic we broke new ground.

Looking back now, I realize that the most fundamental decision that we made in the early years emerged from a protracted argument about the organizational structure of the Polytechnic. The essence of the problem was this. Are the units of which a very large place is comprised to be academic units of a traditional and conventional kind, or are they to be units characterized by the activity to which they are leading? In other words, is the institution as a whole composed of disciplines and subjects which can be combined together to form a course for somebody engaging in a career, or is the institution as a whole to be formed from units which are themselves oriented towards practice, towards vocations? In practice this meant that the departments of the Polytechnic must be either subjects — mathematics, physics, chemistry, biology, etc. — or organizations for the running of courses. That was much more fundamental than it may appear at first sight, because the decision gives the key to the character of the institution to which the academic staff belong. After long discussion we opted to base the Polytechnic upon courses. The departments became organizations for the invention, initiation, running, management and examination of courses. This was in line with the reality of the situation. Courses are what students join. They do not come to a polytechnic to study a subject with a view to becoming academics if successful. They come to a polytechnic to engage in jobs which have to do with industry and the professions. It was therefore logical that they should follow a course which was specifically oriented to that end.

With one or two exceptions, caused largely by what we

had inherited, the main one being mathematics which spends most of its time servicing other departments, we therefore organized the Polytechnic as a number of course-based departments, modified later to become Schools. There were eighteen schools, all of which had names which indicated their function, and all of which ran courses which were geared to professional work. It followed from this that in the main the members of the Schools would be drawn, not just from one discipline, but from a variety of disciplines.

I would not countenance the idea of faculties which would have tended to concur with the former divisions into the constituent colleges, and would have presented an unassailable barrier both to the development of a total polytechnic ethos, and to the innovative thinking about course-based work which broke the cast-iron moulds in people's minds of higher education conducted through separate and elitist 'quality' disciplines. (I add as a post-script that faculties were introduced to Leeds Polytechnic in 1986 by my successor, Christopher Price, and (as I wryly note) they coincide almost exactly with the constituent colleges of 15 years earlier. History has a way of coming full circle!)

Another decision of importance we made was on the size of the Schools. In an institution the size of the Polytechnic (it was to rise to about 10 000 students full and part-time, and almost 1000 academic staff) it seemed to me essential that the Schools, as the working units to which students and staff would belong, should be of a realistic size for both staff and students to identify with and live and work with. Looked at from my own point of view, it was clear that I could not know my entire staff. It seemed essential to be able to get to know all my heads of schools and something of their family circumstances, and as many as possible of the course directors. Following from Schumacher's ideas of 'small is beautiful', I decided that the optimum size for a

School was about 300 — a big enough socio-academic group for students to recognize and get to know each other without suffering any sensation of the ghetto. With a staff:student ratio of 1:10 this number provided a School board of studies whose maximum size would be 30, even in the unlikely occurrence of everybody turning up for a meeting — the largest number possible in my estimation for any meeting that intends to be productive. That began to solve the immediate problems of organization. But it also raised the question, where was the Polytechnic going? There was perpetual tension between academic respectability and devotion to the world of work. What is now known as 'academic drift' goes in the direction of academic respectability. We were set up to do something more serious, more immediate, and I soon realized, more difficult. For as I slowly recognized after a lot of discussion and thinking, we were actually engaged in a major educational revolution of the utmost significance for the country. The fact that I had not noticed it before — and that most of my former colleagues, in universities and schools, could not imagine what I was talking about — was caused by our inability to imagine that anything could possibly be wrong with our educational system. Of course, people criticized it and constantly proposed developments, usually reorganization of some kind, which gives people the illusion of making progress while actually going on teaching the same thing. The necessary revolution was much more fundamental and involved the very basis of education. If there was to be a serious change — in the direction of usefulness, of jobs, of activity, of work — the polytechnics must be not just second-choice institutions but the key to the future. That meant recognizing that vocational education and training to the highest possible level must be as estimable as — and more urgently needed than — the conventional studies that are regarded as having the highest status. To put it more simply than the academic mind likes, a production engineer or an industrial designer must be regarded with every bit as much respect, and educated with every bit as much care, as a specialist in English literature, a researcher in chemistry or an historian. But that has never happened since the early nineteenth century. We needed more of the oil can and less of the inkwell.

I did not at first realize how deeply inbred was the status system in education, a matter I shall discuss more fully in Chapter 4. It was pernicious not just because it created social distinctions, but because it actively penalized and discouraged anyone interested in being useful.

So it was important that we teach the right things and try to find out the right way to teach them. The right things were not 'subjects' or 'disciplines', the conventional divisions of learning which make it easy to teach the same things for ever; but *activities*, learning to do something. To take two simple examples, we must teach people to speak and use a foreign language in daily intercourse, both private and commercial, not just learn about foreign literature; we must train people to be social workers, not just study sociology. We must give people skills, not just the ability to appreciate and criticize.

This approach affected the provision of facilities within the actual Polytechnic buildings. For our teaching must be conducted in and through workshops, studios and laboratories, as much as in classrooms; our library must not just be storage space for the products of past minds, but must be a resource centre providing access to necessary information, ideas and methods and materials.

The general orientation of our studies had to be action; they might be pursued by action learning. A polytechnic, I decided, using its correct meaning as a guide, was an institution (and perhaps a community) for the development and teaching of the practical arts. That required qualities such as clarity of the mind, decisiveness, the ability to work together in groups, practical and manual skills, an understanding of physical reality. The future of our most successful and brilliant graduates would be not to continue in the institution, like a professor in a university, but to get away and become deeply involved in the world of practical affairs.

Everything was against it — the influence of the universities, one or two of which noticed the existence of the polytechnics but did not take them seriously until their teachers were paid nearly as much as their university counterparts, and the attitudes of society, teachers and parents, all conditioned to believe in the status of uselessness. There were clear implications for the kind of studies we ought to pursue. We were concerned not with an elite but with the everyday world, and therefore with the education of Everyman, who has to live there, like it and make it work.

These considerations led naturally to an emphasis on teaching in the Polytechnic rather than research. I will comment later, in Chapter 3, on the dominance of research in universities and the role it plays in the academic ethos. In the early days of the Polytechnic I used to make light-hearted cracks in my speeches to the effect that what many universities called 'research', we in the polytechnic world called 'reading books', 'working in the lab or studio', or even simply 'keeping up with my subject'. These were activities I expected of myself and my staff, not so that they could bring glory on themselves and Leeds Polytechnic by publishing or acquiring post-graduate degrees, but simply because they were essential if we were continually to improve the quality of our teaching. With this end in view, I set up within the Polytechnic a unit known as the Educational Technology Unit whose business it was not simply to invent, make and maintain teaching machines and video and recording equipment, but to liaise with the library resource centre in originating all sorts of methods to improve teaching. It was to be a service unit helping to improve, and if necessary transform, the standard of teaching, so that the Polytechnic would become the best *teaching* institution in the country!

The problems of the Polytechnic became more acute with the events from 1973 onwards. About that time it was recognized by the government that the birthrate had in fact been dropping since 1965, and that there would not be enough pupils to enter the schools to employ the staff who were already trained and about to be trained by the colleges of education. The solution to this was at first muddled and confused, and in many ways unsatisfactory. What it meant in practice for us was that the teacher training colleges in Leeds, with the exception of anything in the University, were amalgamated with the Polytechnic which now became a larger and more comprehensive organization, still geared to courses aimed at vocations (one of which was teacher training), but wider in its scope and infinitely more complex in the motives of its students and in popular esteem.

Teacher training poses many of the problems of higher education, because it is the link between schools of all levels and higher education at all levels. In the great expansion of the 1960s the teacher training colleges had tried to become something like mini-universities. Because of the organization of subjects in the schools along traditional lines — English, history, geography, physics, chemistry, biology, etc.— it seemed obvious to organize the teacher training colleges along the same lines with, of course, a little training in teaching methods and more in the theory of education, the history of education, the psychology of education, and so on. Because of that, and because in any case their courses were validated by the universities, they followed a pattern which was more typical of the universities than of anything else.

The joining of the teacher training colleges with the polytechnics meant, in the case of those polytechnics which had thought the matter out, a fundamental revolution in their way of thinking. If the teacher training section was to draw upon the polytechnic's expertise as a whole, and if its students were to become part of the community of learning for work, it followed that the courses and the areas of expertise in which the future schoolteachers were trained, were unlikely to be exactly the same as those of the former colleges and the existing universities.

But that meant that the teachers likely to be produced by a polytechnic school of education might not be exactly matched to the conventional needs of the schools. Was it likely that the needs of the schools would change? The fact is that it was absolutely essential that they should change – and essential precisely because schools were by political decision becoming comprehensive. If comprehensive schooling was to mean anything other than a political flag and the existence of institutions in which the grammar school pupils would do well and the others would be consigned to the back of the class to bide their time and become discontented, it must be because the schools would sooner or later see their way to establishing, at the same level as the more conventional academic studies, work and activities for the boys and girls in the school which would lead them directly and meaningfully into the world of work. That, it seemed to me, was where the enlarged polytechnics should belong. Of course, it was not as simple as that. The polytechnics were (and still are) part of the minority provision, catering for the less than 20 per cent that go on to higher education. If the polytechnics were to offer, as they theoretically did, an alternative to the universities, they must offer an education and training that was wider than that. They should be genuinely comprehensive. At the least they should be essential components of a system of higher education, able to meet the needs of the boys and girls coming from comprehensive schooling. That would only make sense if higher education were seen as comprehensive at its own level. The part to be played by the polytechnics seemed to me clear. Polytechnics, like the majority in the schools, must be concerned with action, with training people for work in its widest sense, with the world (and the culture of) doing and making.

In the 150 years following the Industrial Revolution we had contrived to create an educational system least suited to the actual needs of society, of industry and the professions. To understand that, and to find a key to our present problems, it is essential to look at that tradition, at the beliefs and values established in the nineteenth century and the response of the educational establishment to the Industrial Revolution and its aftermath.

PART 2
THE PROBLEM

3 Learning for its Own Sake

It should be impossible to discuss the educational system of today without recognizing the fundamental changes in intellectual and personal horizons made by the Industrial Revolution and its aftermath. The fact that at least in principle we are no longer concerned with education and training for a minority but with education and training for everyone is the result of the Industrial Revolution and the urban revolution that accompanied it. Those movements opened up huge new areas of work, new possibilities for invention and design, new sources of power; they demanded new skills and new aspirations. And they threw into prominence new people. They came from all sorts of backgrounds, geographical and social, and were various in character and attainment. But they did have this in common — that, by and large, *the pioneers of the new processes and manufactures that made the Industrial Revolution possible were not known for their education.* To take a few major historical figures — the Arkwrights, Brindley, Telford, Stephenson and other innovators in the field of education itself — they managed more than well despite that conspicuous disadvantage. It may even be that their lack of formal — and certainly any kind of higher — education was a benefit. They could look at a problem direct, assess it without preconceptions, devise original ways of answering it, create artefacts without aesthetic prejudice, and call upon new skills, usually at first without training.

The schools gradually set up to provide that training were essentially practical and based upon work — not upon an appreciation of what it might be like to work, but as an aid to people already doing it. The first Mechanics' Institutes were set up in the 1820s. Between that and the Technical Instruction Act 1889 they had mixed fortunes and many discouragements, in notable contrast with their equivalents on the continent. But as they haltingly developed — into colleges and institutes of technology and art — they were essentially part-time and often evening schools, where people from work could more conveniently be taught by experienced people also from work the skills that they needed and others that they might need for the future. That is not to describe an ideal system to be reviewed with nostalgia; it is merely to point to an important characteristic of practical education — that *the best way to learn a thing is to do it*.

A convenient moment at which to appreciate what happened in England is 1851. In that year the Great Exhibition brought people — not only bystanders but industrial entrepreneurs — from all over the world to see in the exhibition (and in the industrial cities) not only the peculiarities of contemporary Victorian taste but the practical effects of the Industrial Revolution that Britain had pioneered. It was a fitting culmination to a century of invention and change. For the hundred years from 1750 to 1850 were the formative period of the Industrial Revolution, starting in the hills and valleys of Britain, spreading to Europe and ultimately affecting the whole world. The visitors to the Great Exhibition did not just look with wonder; they studied what had happened and took the knowledge back to their own countries to develop processes often initiated in Great Britain. They did so just as this country was doing it best to turn its back upon the very discoveries and processes that had made it the crucible of the new age. The Europeans not only followed the manufactures and processes; they took a hard look at the way people were being trained to use them. And having already the beginnings of a system of education relevant to the needs of industrial society, they elaborated it. Two years after the exhibition, Dr Lyon Playfair, having studied industrial education in Europe, reported that industry there was bound to overtake Britain if Britain failed to alter its outlook and methods.

The European countries had every reason to proceed with confidence. In contrast to our halting and never full-blooded attempts to set up a few classes in technical instruction, with the Mechanic's Institutes, some part-time studies and eventually local colleges of technology, the European countries had already been establishing powerful places of learning and instruction, serious institutions for the study and practice of technology at the highest level.

The French *École Polytechnique*, still one of the most prestigious centres of education in Europe, was founded in 1794. It should be noted that it was set up to train not only key administrators but also skilled experts in engineering and public works; and it was accompanied by a new *Conservatoire des Arts and Métiers*. The *Polytechnische Institut* of Vienna was founded in 1815; the *Technische Hochschule* at Karlsruhe in 1825; the schools at Dresden in 1828 and Stuttgart in 1829. It took until 1890 before they could grant their own degrees but by 1851 they were already institutions of senior rank. The most celebrated of the polytechnics in Europe was the *Zurich Polytecknikum* founded in 1855. That influenced Germany in particular and it was Germany that influenced America. In America, the Massachusetts Institute of Technology was founded in 1865.

It is significant that *in every country in which technical education was taken seriously its development was accompanied by a system of national education* – a recognition of the elementary fact that if they were to play a part in the changing world *everyone* must have instruction in reading and writing and counting.

The contrast with England was many times recorded and equally often ignored. After Britain's disastrously poor performance at the Paris Exhibition of 1867, Dr Lyon Playfair again wrote, in a letter quoted in *The Times*:

> Deficient representation in some of the industries might have accounted for this judgement against us, but when we find that out of 90 classes there are scarcely a dozen in which pre-eminence is unhesitatingly awarded to us, this plea must be abandoned ... So far as I could gather them by conversation, the one cause upon which there was most unanimity of conviction is that France, Prussia, Austria, Belgium, and Switzerland possess good systems of industrial education for the masters and managers of factories and workshops, and that England possesses none.

It was not only Lyon Playfair. Thirty years later the Royal Commission on Technical Education of 1884 emphasized the superiority of German over English school education and the general level of ignorance in England among working people. Forster's Education Act had made it possible for money to be provided out of the rates to set up new schools and in 1880 primary education had become compulsory. But it was not until 1902 that the new Education Act initiated a coherent system of state secondary education. Even after that it was many years before the majority of children stayed at school beyond the age of fourteen.

In the technical field the Technical Instruction Act 1889 authorized local authorities to use for technical education the produce of a penny rate. There were a few technical colleges; a handful of polytechnics in London, a few exceptions in the North of England like the colleges of the 1870s to 1890s which were in the early 1900s to become the great civic universities of Manchester, Leeds and Liverpool. The Imperial College of Science and Technology was founded in 1903. But apart from that there were in the early years of the twentieth century only 31 technical schools, with fewer than 3000 students between them. Of the universities, only Edinburgh indulged in a brief flirtation with technology with the appointment of George Wilson, a remarkable man qualified in both medicine and chemistry, to a Chair of Technology in 1855. He was however the first and last holder of the Chair.

Looking at the situation dispassionately, it must be concluded that the reluctance of Britain to develop a coherent system of technical education rested upon a deeply-rooted dislike of technology — and therefore of the developing world. The attitude of the people developing the educational system was not to exploit that world but in some way to correct it, to provide answers to it. In that sense it was a development, not of excitement and wonder, but of fear. In the light of the history of this country it is all the more extraordinary that that should have happened. It was not, I believe, the result of something inherent in the national character but a direct response, by the intelligentsia, the professors, the clergy and the gentry, to the urgent and demanding world of the industrial revolution. It should, after all, have been easy to build upon the fascination with science of the seventeenth century, the spirit of the founders of the Royal Society, the conviction that men were becoming the masters and possessors of nature: or upon the Enlightenment of the eighteenth century when men of genius, in Whitehead's words, 'applied the seventeenth century group of scientific abstractions to the analysis of the unbounded universe'. In the event, that excitement became more rarefied, and distinct from the everyday world of technological change. And the mainstream of the intellectual world moved away from the industrial world altogether. It was at heart a retreat – a retreat from reality. And it found its shelter appropriately, in the cloisters of Oxford.

Three figures of nineteenth-century Oxford will suffice as representative of the educational ethos. Mark Pattison is usually accepted as the prototype for Mr Casaubon, the pedant in George Eliot's *Middlemarch*. In fact, Pattison swung between pedantry and a revival of standards of scholarship and teaching at a time when Oxford was badly in need of it. But he remains a symbol – almost the type – of academic scholarship and personal remoteness, obsessed with and utterly absorbed by the minutiae of the intellectual life.

More creatively, Newman represents – and in his *Idea of a University* specifically set out – ideals of university education, and thus of education as a whole. Central to that approach was the idea of education as an end in itself, untouched at its highest and best by having to make a thing or earn a living.

This process of training, by which the intellect, instead of being formed or sacrificed to some particular or accidental purpose, some specific trade or profession, or study or science, is disciplined for its own sake, for the perception of its own proper object, and for its own higher culture, is called liberal education; and though there is no one in whom it is carried as far as is conceivable, or whose intellect would be a pattern of what intellects should be made, yet there is scarcely anyone but may gain an idea of what real training is, and at least look towards it, and make its true scope and result, not something else, his standard of excellence; and numbers there are who may submit themselves to it, and secure it to themselves in good measure. And to set forth the right standard, and to train according to it, and to help forward all students towards it according to their various capacities, this I conceive to be the business of a university.

That is a sentiment wholly admirable and appropriate for its time. To us, looking back at the situation now, it seems that Newman was more precisely reflecting the irony of his time than he himself imagined. For he wrote at a critical moment when the impact of the industrial revolution was transforming society. To him the answer to that problem lay in a liberal education. But it involved withdrawing from the ordinary, unacceptable, degrading environment of work that the Industrial Revolution was responsible for producing. As the population crowded into monstrous cities and multiplied, the life of the mind was seen to withdraw to the attractive, leisurely and genteel surroundings of Oxford and Cambridge. A university education became again, what it has always had a natural tendency to become, at once refined and profound and remote from the crude realities of urban life.

But the most immediately influential statement establishing the ethos of an educated and cultured elite dominating the whole field of learning and society, was Matthew Arnold's *Culture and Anarchy*. Arnold's influence was wide; he was, after all, both an academic and, for most of his career, an Inspector of Schools. The book, as he later remarked, was one of the only books to have become a classic in the lifetime of its author; and that was because Arnold found words to give his readers an instant recognition of the intellectual issues of their time. Central to the argument was the fundamental assumption which gives the title to the book. Anarchy was the world of industry and machines and therefore of dehumanization; culture was the corrective, the answer to it; and the signs of culture were sweetness and light. For culture

> does not try to teach down to the level of inferior classes; it does not try to win them for this or that sect of its own, with ready made judgements and watch words. It seeks to do away with classes; to make the best that has been thought and known in the world current everywhere; to make all men live in an atmosphere of sweetness and light, where they may use ideas, as it uses them itself, freely — nourished and not bound by them.'

With one intellectual leap, Arnold established the ethos of the middle classes and did so in the same decade as Forster's Education Act. It was of course a help in becoming a man of culture if you had a reasonable income already or earned one on the side; but what was clear was that the act of making, a deep involvement with design and technology, could not be a route to culture. *The great divide between enlightenment and work was now designated and preserved.* It would be many years, if ever, before the gulf could be bridged between education and work.

Those three intellectual expositors, even the many people influenced by them, could not however have established such a complete and lasting outfit of social and educational values if their work had not been reinforced by a conscious or unconscious acceptance of a profound philosophical system. What underlay that intellectual movement was the thought of Plato, and specifically the revival of his thought in the nineteenth century. It is difficult to exaggerate the importance of this intellectual substratum. It affected in the most fundamental way the entire educational world. And it still does. For *the profound attraction of Plato's thought was to offer the intellectual an escape from the mundane world of everyday work and living.* Reality was not in that world; reality was in the world of Forms or Ideas, to which the everyday world was a more or less successful approximation. What a wonderful piece of sleight of mind, turning things upside down and finding the most respectable philosophical justification for the privileged world of leisure, discussion and speculation – a pure world of clear and perfect unities not to be found in the imperfect, flawed and confused world of industry and work.

Plato is the ultimate authority for the nineteenth- and twentieth- century concept, or ideal, of a liberal education. What he was not responsible for was that it became a stranglehold upon the whole system. It did so because it neatly fitted the hierarchical character of British society. A liberal education became the peak to which an education should aspire. *The ordinary mind dealt with things; the educated mind dealt in ideas.* And that had a profound effect upon the most influential institutions.

There seem to be periods in the life of all institutions when their leaders turn in upon themselves and concentrate upon their own self-improvement and self-preservation rather than the service they do to the outside world. Society may now and again hammer upon the door and shout for them to come out and lend a hand in the street; usually there is no answer. Withdrawal from everyday affairs is a constant temptation of the academic world, usually in the universities, today possibly in the polytechnics; *everyday realities are so much less simple than the contemplation of eternal truths.* And where better to contemplate them than in the universities, first the ancient colleges of Oxford and Cambridge, then in the provincial universities, founded as colleges for practical training and quickly celebrating their admission into the higher world of learning. Increasingly, with every year, through the nineteenth and twentieth centuries, the universities and the essential university ethos came to dominate the whole of education. They were the peak, they set the standard, they were a magic world to which the fortunate might one day be admitted.

To make sure of this and fill a gap that might have remained in the circle of education, the government took a decision in 1917 that was to have the most permanent and drastic effect upon the fortunes of the country. In that year the government, in an attempt to rationalize and give some order to the chaos of school-leaving examinations, decreed that the universities would be responsible for conducting school leaving examinations. The system was now complete. For, although it was emphasized by the Board of Education that it should be 'a cardinal principle that the examinations should follow a curriculum and not determine it', in practice the very opposite happened. The examinations and their requirements became the key to studies in secondary schools. They also became something more. The examinations were supposed to be school-leaving examinations; they inevitably became qualifying examinations for entry to the universities. And that had a profound effect upon the whole orientation of studies and teaching. It made entry to the universities the highest aspiration for teachers and pupils, and thus had a profound bearing upon the subjects which would be taught, their nature and scope, and the character of the educational experience of the pupils. For it followed from that simple decision that the ethos of the university should become fundamental to the whole of education and training. And what did the universities deal in? Not training for a job, not developing skills in design and making, not encouraging action; they dealt in learning, grouped into subjects and disciplines and neatly compartmented according to the subject rather than the needs of people or society.

So education became the assembly of subjects and then,

at the higher level, disciplines. They, like Platonic forms, had their own essence and boundaries; they were to be handed on, or such parts of them as seemed reasonable to communicate. And what kept them in good shape was more and more study of them, becoming more specialized with every year and eventually, under the influence of Germany and America, receiving the delectable accolade of research. The academic factory was now in business, sufficient unto itself; research, including literary research about matters so uninteresting that no one was likely to want to do it again, became the aim of the learned and teaching a poor second, not indeed what the professors were really there to do. Among that research a small proportion was of the utmost significance for the future of the world. But for the most part, the material poured in and out, weighing down the library floor, becoming sooner or later itself the stuff for more research and more papers.

That tradition – and especially the conventional acceptance of what Whitehead called 'inert knowledge' – is so general and established that it still inspires and underlies almost all educational thinking. To take one recent example, there was issued in 1977 a discussion initiated by the Prime Minister, James Callaghan, known as the Great Debate and brought together as a Green Paper under the title *Education in Schools: A Consultative Document*. Shirley Williams, the Secretary of State for Education, hosted public meetings throughout the country.

As a well-written summary of a mass of debate by some of the best people in education, it is a document remarkable for its conventionality and its complacency. It is, of course, oriented towards educational administration and politics rather than teaching. But what in the context of this chapter is particularly fascinating is the list of aims of the schools which 'the majority of people would probably agree with'. Out of eight wordy aims, only one contains — in a phrase tacked on at the end, 'giving them the ability ... to apply themselves to tasks' — a hint that it might be good for children to learn to *do* something. There is a reference to engaging in work in primary schools as part of the 'child-centred' approach; but generally education is seen to need more standard assessment and an agreed secondary curriculum for all pupils. And what that education really consists of is information, critical discussion and appreciation of the mixed economy, the political system and the wealth creating parts of industry. There was no reference to working as part of a team. Supporting it all is the substratum of conventional, accepted values. The gifted will go on to academic studies; the less gifted will turn their attention to careers and the world of work, presumably earning enough to keep the gifted in study. There is no hint that it might be good for the gifted to enter work at the sharp end, and not even a suspicion that there might be something to be said for learning to do things, to make things, to invent, to wonder, to discover the fascination of nature and things and the fantastic possibilities in doing and making. Even though it is familiar knowledge that if you want to cultivate a habit or a skill or an attitude, you must start it early, it seems to have been forgotten that the conventional kind of schooling might be re-examined, to ask at least if there might be a more real and fundamental way of learning to take part in an urban industrial society than just to add to the curriculum a few classes on appreciation.

And yet, as I have already emphasized, there has been no shortage of people commenting on the dangers inherent in our attitudes and warning us of what might happen — warnings that now seem only too perceptive of the reality that would overtake us. Over a hundred years ago, in 1869, Herbert Spencer wrote:

That which our school-courses leave almost entirely out, we thus find to be what most nearly concerns the business of life. Our industries would cease, were it not for the information which men acquire, as best they may, after their education is said to be finished. The vital knowledge — that by which we have grown as a nation to what we are, and which now underlies our whole existence — is a knowledge that has got itself taught in nooks and corners, while the ordained agencies for teaching have been mumbling little else but dead formulae.'

4 A Contemporary Crisis: The Problem of Status

Before starting to build up the framework for a more relevant and realistic approach to education it is essential to emphasize a specifically English problem that grew larger with every episode mentioned in the last chapter and which today complicates every attempt to reform or improve the system. It might formerly have been described as the problem of class distinction; it is now better described as the problem of *status*. We belong to a stratified society and that has a profound bearing on education. It can be expressed this way. *In a hierarchical society, the status of education rises from common utility at the bottom to personal satisfaction at the top.* Whatever the state of mind of the teachers and pupils in less privileged schools, there can be no doubt about the status and privileged life of the university professor, especially one who specializes in research.

Personal satisfaction may, of course, be the starting-point for discovery and invention, especially in the arts and pure sciences; it has often been so in history. It may even be that some of the most significant technological developments of our time were the outcome of isolated episodes of research for its own sake. But personal satisfaction usually has little effect on technology and is not always within the reach of Everyman.

Why does education lead so easily to isolation? There seems to be some factor in the actual process of learning and teaching that turns education in on itself. It may be caused by the subject boundaries, by a longing for the neatness of compartmentalized knowledge, or a preference for the relatively ordered world of research rather than the changing and uncomfortable world of ordinary work. The process of learning itself encourages isolation. But it is even more fundamental. Underlying everything else in our educational system is an assumption which starts in the secondary schools and grows from that point — that education is ultimately for the isolated and unique individual self. The whole curriculum is devised to that end — self-recognition, self-awareness, self-expression. To the ultimate implications of that I shall return later. For the moment it is only necessary to insist that it has been a continuous and accelerating process. There has been no shortage of attempts to correct the situation in the last 100 years. There have been many experiments in schools, and a mass of studies and reports; institutions have been founded to bring education back to reality, like the Royal College of Art which was set up to train designers for industry. Attempts to remind it of its intended role have generally failed.

Despite that wealth of thinking and experiment little seems to have changed. The status system looks like surviving indefinitely. In the field of higher education, the status of universities is pre-eminent and universities themselves are graded in public esteem. However rigorous their examinations and high the standard of their degrees, the polytechnics are of lower status than the universities. Now, when they are beginning to get their heads above the water, they are still, in the view of many schools and parents, second-choice institutions; and there is still pressure upon them — from outside as well as from many of their own academic staff – to become as like the universities as possible.

Now I want to take the argument a little further. Those distinctions rest upon a peculiarly British foundation. There is in Britain a deeply ingrained belief that practical people must be stupid. It is a belief that is not changed by the creation of mixed-ability classes in comprehensive schools. It is still assumed that the brighter will go on to further study and the dimmer will do practical tasks. It rests upon two basic assumptions – that the brighter pupils will always want to move away from work and that brightness is of a certain kind – that is, verbal and numerical. We are trapped in a net of conventional ideas about brightness and cleverness. What is required is a radical reassessment of what we mean by cleverness and stupidity; for our conventional ideas may be wrong and, I believe, are in fact wrong for our society and for its work. *In an advanced technological society there should be different ways of grading cleverness and stupidity, recognizing the excitement and satisfaction to be had in activity and the real abilities needed in work.* We could make a start in changing attitudes by banning the use of the word 'able' by teachers and educationists. As it is used in common parlance, 'able' means verbally and numerically able; the 'less able' child is the child whose talents do not lie within the sphere of conventional academic disciplines. Sir Alex Smith, former Director of Manchester Polytechnic, used to tell a very good story of how, when he was visiting a school, he came across a most superb scale model of a boat. He stopped to admire it, and the headmaster said what a pity it was that the boy who had made it was one of their least able children. The story speaks for itself.

Where do these assumptions originate? The problem starts at the very beginning of the educational experience, and becomes acute at the moment we differentiate learning from ordinary living: the divorce between living and learning happens in the secondary schools.

There is a fundamental connection between learning and living, and a mountain of evidence to confirm it. We recognize it in our primary schools and know it from our own experience – that doing and learning are intimately related. The thinking of Illich on deschooling society may provide no answer to our particular predicament but it is based upon a known truth about people. Education starts in living. Much of it is subsequently affected by the process of learning as well as by its content.

What happens? That wonderful mixture of life, learning, family, fun, playing and studying comes at the beginning. *At its best it is not just permissiveness or lack of discipline but a controlled unity of living and learning.* But there is a dramatic change as soon as the pupils enter secondary education. The schools are bigger; that enables them to have better facilities and a wider range of subjects for 'A' levels. But the change is more fundamental than that. It is a change to another mode of learning. For now it is a world of handed-down culture, of information, of exercises that become increasingly sophisticated, a world that revolves around the teaching of generalizations – principles, rules, laws, probabilities. In terms of scholarship that may well be right. But in human terms, teaching has been turned upside down. Where previously the pupils' own experience led towards the forming of generalizations, now generalizations are followed (luck and time permitting) by practice, and so may or may not lead back to experience. The classroom takes the place of the playroom, studio or workshop. Even where some attempt has been made to give recognition to the value of practical subjects such as woodwork or domestic science, the examination system often makes the last state worse than the first. For to raise the status of a practical subject, it is made examinable, and a theoretical syllabus is worked out accordingly. Thus Domestic Science has become Home Economics, a subject so laden with theories of chemistry and hygiene and nutrition that I have encountered children totally turned off the subject because they had not been permitted to leave their notebooks and pens and so much as approach a mixing bowl or a cooker throughout their entire first term; and those who achieve the high flights of taking the subject at higher levels have informed me gravely that they are not just cooks and are proud of the fact that their last two years of sixth-form studies have been almost entirely on paper.

For this is where the status race begins. The brightest are those who respond most easily to this mode of learning; the dimmest are those who learn from doing and making. In fact, it is a circular situation. *The secondary system discovers the brightest children. The brightest children are those who are discovered by the secondary system.* By the age of 13 or 14 we have already divided them into those moving towards learning and those moving towards work. The key to their status is whether they are likely to go to university. Ask any boy or girl of 13 upwards. Despite all the experiments of this century, despite many experiments in teaching and learning, despite the hours spent in teacher-training colleges studying the psychology of learning, the irony is that we are more obsessed with examinations than ever before. And it is getting worse.

What are schools for?	Passing examinations
What are examinations for?	Getting into university
What are universities for?	Getting degrees
What are degrees for?	Staying in the university if you get a good one

Somewhere on the edge of the path or slipping between its paving-stones or striding off in a different direction, are people who enter instead the world of work to earn enough money to support the people who stay on at the university or polytechnic. Yet these people who slip off the royal road are the majority. They are the citizens of our society. Without them, the country would come to a halt. There would be no culture, no universities, no polytechnics.

The introduction of one leaving examination for all pupils (GCSE in England and Wales; Standard Grade in Scotland) lights a torch of hope for those who feel this to be a matter of urgency. But already voices of doubt are being raised. The very flexibility of the new exams allow for the new direction towards practicality to be side-stepped. Many teachers, parents and even children are very conservative: they like the familiarity of the old ways, and disguise their lack of energy for innovation behind warning cries about a drop in standards. The same pressures are likely to remain – for core curricula, standard subjects, standard examinations, and pieces of paper for everyone. Behind it all still lies the same pressure to get into a university. There is nothing the matter with that in itself. It is an admirable ambition. For the university is crucial to our society. Not just to its educational structure; to its whole ethos. For the universities are the safeguards of our freedom, dedicated to the pursuit of knowledge wherever it may lead, however uncomfortable the consequence. Even if we did not need them for education, we would need them for establishing intellectual standards and transmitting culture. They are centres of consciousness for our civilization. *But while that is essential to our kind of society, it is a function not sufficiently general to shape the whole of education.* There is no doubt of the influence that the universities have had upon the whole of education, an influence that, because of the universities' own character in the last century and a half, has bent education in a certain direction.

Sir Alex Smith, the first Director of Manchester Polytechnic, has written clearly and sympathetically about the situation:

> The university model gives pride of place to intellectual excellence, but it is weakened and distorted when it is diluted and when it tries to do something for which it is unsuited, by background, experience and ethos. The pre-eminence given to this model of higher education has two very damaging effects in our society. First it generates a hierarchy of esteem in which other very legitimate and praiseworthy educational aims are deemed to be less significant. Secondly it generates a similarly misguided hierarchy of esteem in which human activities are graded — arts is reckoned superior to science, science superior to applied science, applied science superior to technology, technology superior to engineering, design engineering superior to production engineering.
>
> The university model has other implications. It leads to knowledge being separated into suitable subject areas — history, philosophy, mathematics, physics, chemistry and so on — and these are studied in great depth in departments comparatively isolated from the interaction of other subject areas.

That may, of course, be right for many students and many academic staff. The problem is not with the universities as such, or even necessarily with that university model. The problem is the belief that everyone should go to a university if possible. The university ethos may even be irrelevant to many of the boys and girls who do go to one. The best statement I know about the objectives of the students is that given in paragraphs 107 and 108 of the White paper, *Education: a framework for expansion* (1972) that was published when Margaret Thatcher was Secretary of State for Education and Science:

> The motives that impel sixth formers to seek higher education are many, varied and seldom clear-cut. A minority wish to

continue for its own sake the study in depth of a specialised subject to the top of their bent. It is crucial for the world of scholarship, research and invention that their needs should be met. This has always been a leading function of the universities and must remain so. Some students have a specific career in mind. A larger number are anxious to develop over a wider field what the Robbins Committee called the general powers of the mind, but not without questioning whether a specialised honours degree course is the best way of achieving it.

Some ask for no more than a stimulating opportunity to come to terms with themselves, and to discover where their real interests and abilities lie. Others have no better reason than involuntarily to fall in with the advice of their teachers and the example of their contemporaries. But not far from the surface of most candidates' minds is the tacit belief that higher education will go far to guarantee them a better job. All expect it to prepare them to cope more successfully with the problems that will confront them in their personal, social and working lives.

It is important that the last and most widespread of these expectations should not be disappointed. The Government have sympathy with the sincere desire on the part of a growing number of students to be given more help in acquiring — and discovering how to apply — knowledge and skills related more directly to the decisions that will face them in their careers and in the world of personal and social action.

The status system is against them. Even so, some — it may be an increasing number — will choose to come closer to the world of work. And that can only be for the good. The problem of status only disappears when people are working constructively and effectively together towards a common end which is outside themselves. That gives a new dimension to their own experience and their own personalities. It is one of the ultimate lessons for education.

5 The World of Work

It follows from the argument at the end of the last chapter that I should now turn to the world of work — or more specifically to what I mean by the world of work. It will be obvious that I am not speaking only of manufacturing industry, however crucial to our economic life that may be. In the world of work I include the professions, the social services, the personal services, the creative and practical arts — *the whole variegated tapestry of human endeavour*. I only want to isolate a few themes from it, selected because of their significance to any argument about education.

First, *work is not coming to an end*. We now know that there will be permanent structural unemployment; it was inevitable given our socio-economic system and our narrow view of the meaning of work. It increased because advances in modern technology make it unnecessary for many routine tasks to be carried out by people. With a succession of industrial revolutions the situation will not correct itself; *unemployment as presently understood will increase*. I cannot find that anything but good if it means reducing working hours and eliminating the most boring and undignified of jobs. Despite the present unemployment, I do not believe either that work as such will come to an end or that work will become any less significant. The fact is that work is central to a person's status in society and is what gives him or her both a place and an identity. That does not mean that there should be more work or less work, or what kind of work. It implies simply that *we have not yet discovered any alternative to work* — whatever we mean by it — in enabling people to find themselves and develop their relationship to others.

Secondly, the current industrial revolution can be interpreted as reversing many of the trends of the first one. This is mainly due to the fantastic developments in electronics — computers, microprocessors, the applications of semiconductors, the growing family of gadgets becoming cheaper and more readily available to everyone. And they are not merely a technological wonder, they are also an artistic one. For me, the sight of an integrated circuit through a microscope is as vivid as many a more traditional artistic experience. And it is a world which stretches the imagination because it challenges the mind to unprecedented concepts of scale, of infinite bigness and almost infinite smallness. The new industrial revolution has to do with communications and control. Its implications are that there will be more possibilities for the individual, more variability and less routine work. If the first industrial revolution led to the repetition of the assembly-line, now we are in a world where there will be fewer jobs of that sort, but a number of new jobs designing, making and supplying the very artefacts that make routine work unnecessary. And that means a major shift in the meaning and scope of work as a whole.

Thirdly, what we are witnessing does not take away from the need for individual initiatives. It actually increases the need for individuals of capacity, with powers of invention, the ability to pursue, discover and develop things, and the imagination to see potentials everywhere. And that is not only an exciting prospect, but something of the utmost importance for our social and industrial life. *Without creative personal innovations, all work tends towards uniform mediocrity.*

Let me bring these points together and put the argument

in a different way. The technological advances of the last few years mean that it is no longer possible to regard work in a limited way. The term tends to be used for manual or routine work or paid employment; in a modern technological society we are talking of a much more varied group of activities. We may even need a new word to indicate the wider concept of work. Words from the Latin base *labor* either sound too heavy as do those from the German-based *werk*, or else have party political or obstetrical connotations. 'Occupation' indicates a particular role. We have toyed with phrases like 'directed activity' or 'creativity' or even one's 'doings'. None is satisfactory. Perhaps the current jargon 'doing one's own thing' (we shall talk about *things* in a later chapter) or being 'into' something are struggling, as we are, to find a new term for a wider view of work. A rather clumsy formulation is the phrase I used earlier – the whole variegated tapestry of human endeavour. I want to introduce another.

We have, as I outlined in Chapter 3, inherited from Victorian England the divorce between industry and education. Bringing them together requires a recognition of changes in the meaning of work. It is a change not just from labour to leisure but a total view of work, which includes what at the moment look like leisure and leisure activities. Any new, enlarged meaning of work must include welfare, commitment and social concern. We live in what might even become a DIY society, in which everyone will have to do his or her own maintenance and have more personal concern for their immediate environment. In such a situation leisure is not idleness but is part of work, like amateur drama. The problem is not dividing the two, but discovering the real size of the human groups in which work and leisure become one and life becomes creative. We may find a new identity in a new *synoptic view*.

The idea of a synoptic view is, after all, not new. Apart

from any original meanings it was given an urgency and lasting effectiveness by Sir Patrick Geddes, the founder of modern town planning and himself a geographer, in his insistence in *Cities in Evolution* that it was essential for the planner to bring together all the studies and analyses he had carried out in the various areas of social, economic, industrial and geographic survey — Place, Work, Folk — and discover the potential unity between them. That required, he said, a synoptic view. The argument here about work leads to the same conclusion. We need *a synoptic view of work*, which includes not just employment but also many activities which look like being the activities of unemployment. Some of that is leisure; some of it is very hard work indeed, but work that does not lead to much money and may indeed look like pleasure. That includes most of the creative arts. We have inherited, to put it another way, a work ethic which belongs to the Protestant ethic, analysed and criticized by Tawney and later by Galbraith. That ethic should be obsolete. The availability of a technology that dispenses with many repetitive and sub-human jobs can only be a healthy thing if it leads to a better and more creative use of our time. *The problem is that we have the technology but not the social, political and economic thinking that should go with it.* Not for the first time, invention in the physical field is well ahead of the theorists. The inhabitants of the ivory tower have still to get out of it and find out at first hand what they should be writing about.

What does become clearer in the industrial field with every year is that there is likely to be no salvation in tinkering with the mammoth organizations that we have allowed ourselves to form as a result of financial exploits rather than technological ones. The huge impersonal industrial giant is not the inevitable outcome of the evolution of the processes of work but the opposite; all the realities of the actual work show that there is a limit to the scale of operations which can be understood by ordinary common sense and which can allow for a genuine community of the people engaged in devising, controlling and carrying out the work. What leads to the mergers and amalgamations and ultimately the impersonality of work is finance; what emerges from such takeovers and amalgamations is a management of accountants and financiers who do not and cannot know the technology for which they are responsible (especially if, following the conventional wisdom of the 1950s and 1960s, they have diversified into activities about which they know nothing). It is hardly surprising that the gulf between management and labour gets wider if neither has even the vocabulary to speak to the other.

I have emphasized this a little because it has a direct bearing upon education. As a result, at least partly, of the educational opportunities that we have rightly made available in the last 50 years we are dealing now with a literate and critical workforce in an environment in which it is necessary to agree rather than obey. That in itself demands a *work unit which is the size of the human group*, the group large enough to be effective and offer the skills necessary for the improvement of the job, small enough for its members to know one another (at the very least by name) and for the leaders within it to know each other very well indeed.

It is also the condition for creativity. There is no evidence that I know of in history that huge organizations are creative. In fact, the great empires of the past seem by expansion to have sown the seeds of their own destruction. Where vast organizations have succeeded it seems always to be the case that the organization has been broken down internally into creative groups or units. (Indeed, a MIT Survey of American Industry in 1979 showed that 80 per cent of all new jobs in the USA over a seven-year period were created by firms less than four years old and that very small firms employing less than 20 people generated 66 per cent of all the new jobs in the USA.)

Let me at this point pause to take stock of what the implications are if my arguments so far are at least partly correct. If it is reasonably sized groups which are creative, *education cannot be just for the isolated self but must be concerned with the mutuality of human relationships*. It is in those relationships that it becomes possible to do something together. In the world of modern manufacture and design there is nothing that can be done, other than trivialities, by the totally isolated individual. Even activities that at first sight look personal turn out on examination to require the cooperation of others. The artist today cannot even paint in the isolation of his lonely studio unless someone has made him some paints.

That surely means that education has to be rethought, to get the balance better. And it is not a question of naively abandoning one thing and concentrating on its opposite; the individual and the group are always related and the group is a group of individuals. But in what is the character of the individual found? Although many things may change in the next few years, of one thing we can be reasonably certain for the time being — that there is no way other than work for most people to identify themselves; *the identification with work is what gives most people identity and self-respect*. Conversely, identity is crucial to the doing of work — that is, identity as part of a community.

Admittedly, when people don't need to work they often don't exert themselves to find employment, but it is still a fact that for the great majority of people work is what enables them to identify themselves. Many of our surnames (Wright, Smith, Butcher, Baker, Cooper) once identified a particular man by his work.

Two aspects increasingly common on the work scene are worth mentioning here: that 'work' need not be identified with a product, and that 'work' may be DIY and unpaid — doing for ourselves what previously the work ethic demanded that others should be paid to do for us. The days of Hilaire Belloc's Lord Finchley are over:

Lord Finchley tried to mend the electric light
Himself. It struck him dead: and serve him right!
It is the business of the wealthy man
To give employment to the artisan.

But whether we are concerned with independent or inter-dependent activities, with employment or with leisure, we still need to belong to some kind of working group to give us identity. It seems that individual identity depends not so much on the work done as on being part of a community, of some structure which offers security, not necessarily financial but personal.

Several possibilities emerge from this analysis. It may be that dilettantism is going to become respectable and that one of the effects of enforced leisure will be that self-identity instead of being given by jobs will be given by the development of an intellectual discipline, practical or creative activity or hobby. In any event it remains essential to stress the importance of the self-image which until recently came from the identity of the worker, and to note that it may not come from that now.

For the educator it is impossible to overemphasize the importance of this problem. For *as soon as we begin to look at the nature of work in a new and enlarged way it changes the whole of our attitude to vocational education.* It also challenges us to find a respectable philosophical justification for the new position, maybe not as far-reaching as that of Plato, but one which establishes a way in which we, the possessors of an advanced technological civilization and culture, can think constructively and meaningfully about the modern world. As in the case of the nineteenth-century universities and the Platonic culture, it must be possible to see any new educational pattern as a reflection of some deeper philosophical thinking in the contemporary world. Karl Popper has for many people opened up a new landscape of thinking in which many features and accidents of experience seem to fit into place and have a relationship to one another. If nothing else it offers an escape from the traditional dualism which is irrelevant to our complex and multi-directional world. It also introduces an important new concept.

In Popper's thinking, World 1 is the objective world of material things; World 2 is the subjective world of minds; World 3 is the world of objective structures, products of minds or living creatures which once they are produced exist independently of them. To quote from Bryan Magee's book on *Popper* (1973), of World 3,

> forerunners of this in the animal world are nests built by birds or ants or wasps, honeycombs, spiders' webs, beavers' dams, all of which are highly complicated structures built by the animal outside its own body in order to solve its problems.... Furthermore, some of the animal kingdom's structures are abstract: forms of social organisation, for instance, and patterns of communication. In man, some of the biological characteristics which developed to cope with the environment changed that environment in the most spectacular ways: the human hand is only one example. And man's abstract structures have at all times equalled in scale and degree of elaboration his transformation of the physical environment: language, ethics, law, religion, philosophy, the sciences, the arts, institutions. Like those of animals, only more

so, his creations acquired a central importance in the environment to which he had then to adapt himself, and which therefore shaped him.

Popper's World 3 is an exciting concept which I believe has huge significance for us as educators. For, again in Magee's words, it is 'the world of ideas, art, science, language, ethics, institutions – the whole cultural heritage, in short – in so far as this is encoded and preserved in such World 1 objects as brains, books, machines, films, computers, pictures, and records of every kind.' Popper's is, of course, a philosophical concept wider in itself than what I have given an extended meaning as the world of work; but it indicates the way an educator in a changing institution might usefully think of the world for which we are training our students. We must give as wide as possible an interpretation of the meaning of work. We must recognize that all of us, no matter what our particular pursuits, no matter how cultural appear to be our activities or remote our occupations, need the assurance of the certainty of our work. *And we must see work as part of a changing man-made world in which our very activities change the world we are working in.*

Against that background, of an enlarged way of thinking about work – of human endeavour – I want to come back to the more immediate scene and discuss some implications for education.

The following comments are much influenced by Wilfred Brown, formerly managing director and chairman of the Glacier Metal Company and a Minister of State at the Board of Trade. He emphasized that economic goals are not enough. In an advanced technological society we should be concerned with priorities such as health, security, freedom from anxiety, relationships, status and liberty. These are factors which may lead to economic efficiency; but the aim is not 'full employment' but 'abundant employment' which he described as 'a situation where every member of the working population has a fair opportunity to use his personal capacity to the full extent which he desires on work which interests him and which enables him to earn a wage or salary which is consistent with the earnings of others doing a similar level of work to himself.'

It is obvious that for such a goal to be reached some massive rethinking has to be done. It is overdue. We surely cannot go on indefinitely ignoring the realities of advanced technology and its implications for mankind. As Whitehead wrote in 1923: 'The history of mankind has yet to be seen set in its proper relation to the gathering momentum of technological advance. Within the last hundred years, a developed science has wedded itself to a developed technology and a new epoch has opened.'

The implications for that new epoch are not in fact that we shall all have lots of boring leisure, a situation which seems amazingly remote to some of us. Nor are the implications for education that we should lay on additional extramural lectures on sociology, politics, literature and the history of art so as to enable people to watch more television. This, alas, was what happened in many comprehensive schools' fifth forms during the era of the ROSLA (Raising of the School Leaving Age) children. The challenge is to provide people with skills and the urge to engage in activities which will enable them to affect their environment, to play a part in social life, to do and make — perhaps to learn to enjoy as well as experiencing the enjoyment of learning. A part may be played here, at least for that neglected age-group on the verge (we would hope) of a working life rather than of a life of adult unemployment, by the proposed technical colleges for the inner cities, jointly financed by industry and the Department of Education and Science, which were announced by the Secretary of State, Kenneth Baker, in 1986.

Many such institutions may have to come into being and play their part. We have still a lot to find out. In higher education, if there is to be a mutual and effective relationship between work and education, then the real research appropriate for that part of the educational world which is concerned with the world of work should be about the nature and content of work itself, and about predicting its changes and future needs. What is essential is that we do not turn our backs on work, as intellectuals did in the nineteenth century, and shudder away from it. What our developing society demands is not fear and remoteness but more understanding of what work is, of the mutuality of people and things, of the liberty that work can create or destroy, of the meaning of oneself and others. Academics and teachers need to be more involved with the world of work, not less. For there is a deep identity of work and education at all levels and a similarity in what is needed in the world of work and the world of leisure − the 'commonwealth', in Bernard Shaw's phrase, 'in which work is play and play is life'.

I conclude this chapter with a question. In this enlarged view of work, which is more than employment and certainly more than paid employment, is it possible to identify some of the basic themes, one or two characteristics of *any* kind of work, paid or unpaid, big or small, macro- or micro-scale, innovative or repetitive, that underlie the whole scene? One is the need for mutual relationships in its pursuit. Another − crucial to our future − is that any work worth doing involves problem-solving. The problems may be of all sorts, major and minor, from getting across a river by oneself to building a bridge which will take others across. There is no end to them. What I want to insist on is that worthwhile work, work to be done by human beings and work which needs human beings to do it, involves problem-solving. In our evolution of a new theory of education in subsequent chapters we shall devote some thought to the position of problem-solving in our scheme. In fact, any new view of education must contain an emphasis on problem-solving as a central component. The extraordinary fact — as Tyrrel Burgess, author and teacher, has pointed out — is that for most students problem-solving is virtually omitted; the only problem a student has to solve is the problem of getting a degree at the end of the course.

Another theme we must discuss is: Which skills are so basic that they can be transferred or used as the base from which to develop further skills when (inevitably in our fast-moving and pluralistic society) the needs of society change.

It is with these thoughts about work in our society that we can start building a new theory of education for our times.

PART 3
TOWARDS SOME
SOLUTIONS

6 Things: The Beginning of Learning

In trying to build up a theory and an approach that are more relevant to our world and take into account the crucial role of doing and making, I have to start at the beginning, which is not the existing educational system but the elementary physical reality which it studies and reveals.

The conventional educator may find it odd to start with physical reality (sometimes simply known as 'things') because traditionally that has not been thought of as the stuff of education. Education is about ideas, sometimes about people, essentially about abstractions; even the disciplines into which it is conveniently divided are themselves abstractions, classifications of a lot of material which seems significant because a succession of scholars have knocked it into a shape that becomes either more recognizable with every year or less recognizable, depending on the kind of scholarship expended upon it in the interval. Even in the sciences the educator is more comfortable with basic science and with theory than he is with technology, or the actual objects found or made by man.

The fact is that there is a serious imbalance in our society and education system which is profoundly influential on that society and on the people it educates for leading roles. It has to do with the very beginning of education. The beginning of education, for the vast majority of people in every part of the world, is not an inherited classification of ideas; it is the perception and understanding of their world. But if that is true for a relatively primitive society, it must also be emphasized that of no period or society is it more true than our own. You cannot begin to understand the modern world without some grasp of technology – of the things and processes which it creates and is dependent upon. Yet *a far-reaching characteristic of education in this country in the last 150 years has been the dislike and fear of technology*; for the intelligentsia a repeated desire, not to master it and wonder at it, but to escape from it. The beginning of a relevant education for the modern world must be a deep, critical and informed understanding of the nature of physical reality, not a shrinking from it.

If we, for shorthand reasons, call the physical realities which are the initial objects of study 'things', we can gain some illumination from the *Oxford English Dictionary*. For here we find definitions of *thing* not only as 'an inanimate material object', but also as 'that which is done or to be done; a doing, act, deed, transaction; an event, occurrence, incident; a fact, circumstance, experience'; and also as 'whatever is or may be the object of thought'. This points immediately to a basic link between thoughts and things, between perception and things, between people and things. In our increasingly man-made world, a lot of things start as thoughts. That includes everything to do with innovation and invention. The interrelationship between things and thoughts is therefore complex, profound and never totally divisible. But it may be that we have created for ourselves our own philosophical problem by making a division between things and thought that is only defensible in terms of the dualism of western thought. That philosophical dualism has taken as I discussed in the last chapter a serious knock with the philosophy of Karl Popper. I do not have the background or the ability to discuss that in any detail; what is obvious to me, though, is that Popper provides the philosophical basis on which it is at last possible to talk meaningfully about a world which belongs to neither of the theoretical entities of the dualistic system.

This interrelation of things or physical realities with thought and ideas or concepts is, when one comes to think of it, the very substance of education. This makes the schism between the two even more inexplicable. For how do we know about things? To come to grips with something outside ourselves, it has to be perceived either by observation or in the imagination. And yet it is not an either/or situation, for perception and knowledge of things (whether they be objects or places or people or happenings or thoughts) depend on this intimate interrelationship and interaction of observation with imagination or thought. That is the first point I want to make.

My second goes even further, for frequently between perception and thought occurs an intervention from our side into the area of the 'thing'. There is active interaction between the perceiver and the perceived. For we no longer believe in objects existing statically in time and space; we know that even inanimate objects are changing all the time. Indeed, the only way we know that time passes is by reference to the before and after (a minute ago it was like that, now this) of physical reality changing around us. But if things are changing all the time, that requires thought and imagination on our part even to perceive them, still more to understand them. There is even more. Since the quantum theory was enunciated we know that the very fact of our observing phenomena changes the phenomena. And it is a two-way process: What we perceive changes our perceptions and our powers of perception. This increasingly happens with the use of modern technology. David Attenborough's *Life on Earth*, for instance, has for millions of viewers revealed a reality which we could never experience before, and so opened first our eyes and then our minds to a new view and understanding of life — the very stuff of education.

Even those readers whose minds have fluttered with doubts throughout my preceding paragraphs, will be prepared to consider knowledge the stuff of education. But again I ask, how do we get to know things? Does it not come about through the very interaction between man and physical reality we have been talking about? We find out about things not passively but actively — even drastically. We take things to bits, analyse them, we order them, and manipulate them physically — we chop them up, and heat them, and shine lights on them and stretch them bigger and boil them smaller — any amount of interaction, sometimes quite violent. That learning is active is, said Professor Revans, lecturing to a regional management centre in 1977, an idea 'as old as Mankind itself'. And he went on to quote Sophocles: 'One must learn by doing the thing. You may think you know, but you have no certainty until you try it.'

When at the end of an episode of active exercise of healthy curiosity about our world, we not merely write a report but create something new, we are engaging in the process we call Design. During the time-span when man has lived on earth, this two-way interaction between man and his environment has left its mark on almost everything we see. But for the remotest parts of the earth (and these shrink every year) almost everything in our world has been designed or modified by man. Clearly Design is an activity central to our education, and one we shall explore at greater length later in this book. Here, we need only note that, because the essential material of design is the world of things and its basic processes are active, it is virtually ignored in most school curricula. All this vital arena of learning is at the disposal of our educators if only they would cease to fear and shun technology. It seems to me obvious that far from destroying our perceptions, technology can hugely enlarge the richness and fascination of the world. Things contain the very essence of beauty. The beginning of aesthetic experience, of the experience of beauty, of the rightness of form and the memorability of shape and colour and light, is in the appreciation of things, either natural or man-made. The aesthetic experience of the abstract beauty of ideas or of mathematics comes later because it follows from the appreciation of physical reality. The more exploration goes on, the more natural things are probed and investigated, the more elusive and extraordinary becomes reality. Nature in the sense of space seems to have no end — to offer a reality that we have no way of imagining within the categories of our experience.

But if nature is infinitely big it is also presumably infinitely small. The microscopic investigation of plants does not reveal their smallest components; it reveals still further structures in movement. There is no reason to believe that the exploration need ever end. Nature, it seems, for the scientist seeking facts is like medieval man's concept of God — not only infinitely great but also infinitely small. What an astonishing world of wonder and delight is discovered by the cool observation of the mundane! Here may be a reality more ultimate, more exciting, more significant than most traditional beliefs, more demanding to the mind — that the ordinary things we touch and taste, cut and create are infinite in complexity and delight. And if in nature, so with man-made objects — ever more detailed and fantastic in their capabilities, like the inventions of electronics and other manifestations of man's creative ingenuity.

On the face of it, what could provide a richer and more promising basis for a total education from primary through to senior school and beyond? It offers all the joy and fun of nature in its inexhaustible depth and variety, and at the same time contains a training for work, fundamentally related to activity rather than to inert knowledge: at one with, rather than respectful to, the world of industry, of technology in its widest sense.

The value of this educative material is often recognized in our primary schools. This is the world of the growing child − the world of questions: Why? Where? When? How? − the world of pulling things apart and seeing how things work, of trying out his own physical and mental capacities and abilities, of the building of language which makes reflection and further thought possible. This is the very stuff of taking possession of his world − of getting the keys to his kingdom − surely the very stuff of education. And yet it has been the habit of our system that much of this great adventure of learning is left behind when somewhere between 11 and 13 the child enters secondary school, and simultaneously enters a grey world of abstractions and generalities. Obviously, the ability to cope with generalities is a capacity of the maturer mind which small children are not capable of. My point is that by maintaining this schism between ideas and physical realities, we have placed a desert area at the heart of our learning processes in secondary school, and lost an approach and incentive to living which is vitally necessary in the adult world of work and society. If we are to heal this schism, we must come to understand that technology is not opposite to thinking and understanding; they are partners in the learning process.

'The antithesis between a technical and a liberal education,' according to Whitehead, 'is fallacious. There can be no adequate technical education which is not liberal, and no liberal education which is not technical: that is, no education which does not impart both technique and intellectual vision. In simpler language, education should turn out the pupil with something he knows well and something he can do well.' I would add to that that if he can do something well, he can do so because he knows it well, and if he knows it well, he does so because he has come to grips with the experience of doing it.

7 Technology and Technik

So let us look at technology. If an understanding of physical reality can be the start of wonder and delight, it is also the start of the ability to control the physical world. That is sometimes seen as the function and meaning of technology.

Let me first clear away one common misconception. By technology I do not mean Applied Science. A myth has grown up in recent years that Applied Science and Technology are the same. It is probably the result of the status system I described in an earlier chapter; rubbing shoulders with Science would give Technology a little more respectability in the academic world. Technology is not Applied Science and never was for the simple reason that it started differently. *The origins of technology lie in the solving of practical problems.* In that sense the great engineers — Telford and Stephenson, Brunel and Brindley, as indeed the leading engineers of today, whose work includes some of the greatest wonders of our time — were practical men with a massive dose of common sense, enormous energy and the ability to devise ingenious solutions to definable problems. These are the kind of men I propose to use as examples in my discussion of technology because their work arose initially not from the application of scientific theories and principles to a practical situation, but the opposite. It was the solution to problems that provided the material from which to deduce a scientific principle.

That was generally true of the ancient world as of that of primitive man, the toolmaker. *Technique precedes science.* But it was with the development of science that technique was able to progress; and that was a nineteenth-century phenomenon. As inventions were built upon the work of scientists, and scientific principles were deduced from technological inventions, the two activities increasingly over-lapped and their boundaries became less sharply defined. But essentially they are different. Technology is an activity in its own right, with its own bases, objectives and skills, and, for us citizens in an advanced society, of crucial significance. Technology, to quote Robert M. Pirsig's remarkable bestseller *Zen and the Art of Motorcycle Maintenance,*

> is simply the making of things and the making of things can't by its own nature be ugly or there would be no possibility for beauty in the arts, which also include the making of things. Actually a root word for technology, *techne*, originally *meant* 'art'. The ancient Greeks never separated art from manufacture in their minds, and so never developed separate words for them.

Techne means art and craft; *logos* means word or speech. To the Greeks technology, had they used the formulation, would have meant a discourse upon the arts, pure and applied. For us it has come mainly to mean, from the seventeenth century onwards, the applied arts and more specifically the means and processes, the tools and machines, which are the means to an end — the product. A typically modern view, in the latest edition of the *Encyclopaedia Britannica*, is that technology is 'the means or activity by which man seeks to change or manipulate his environment'. The earlier versions are more helpful because they imply something of the scope of the activity, the universality of its significance, and its essentially creative nature. For me it is a systematic approach to the practical arts. And that has wide ramifications. Wider even than Gordon Childe's account in Singer's *History of Technology*: that technology 'should mean the study of those activities, directed to the satisfaction of human needs, which produce alterations in the material world.'

In particular I want to emphasize, because even technologists often fail to recognize it, that technology requires creativity. Common sense tells us that, in any case. To put it in more current terminology, it includes Design. In the wide and comprehensive way in which I am discussing it, technology can be described as *creative ingenuity*. The phrase is not unusual. But it has been used to considerable effect in articles in *The Times Higher Education Supplement* and other journals in which the author, Michael Fores, has made some provocative points which, with acknowledgement, I wish briefly to summarize.

In Mr Fores' view, the real cultural divide of our day is not that between the well-known 'two cultures' of C.P. Snow, but one between *all* the useful arts and professions on the one hand, and *all* areas of scholarship, including science and the fine arts, on the other — between, in one formulation, technology and the rest. Mankind can be more realistically divided into *homo sapiens*, concerned with reflection and ultimately with wisdom, and *homo faber*, whose concern is with making and using tools to extend his direct and personal powers. *Homo faber* is creative, not because of some instant vision of the kind often attributed to artists (though my own background in art and design does not tell me of many such moments of instant genius) but of long periods of work, struggling with the subject-matter and making useful artefacts as a result of creative activity. He is the creator of products. Whatever field one looks at in the world of contemporary technology, the fact is, in Mr Fores' words, that 'in every case of major technical advance, the most crucial factors have been the pioneer's conception of design and manufacture, of basic need and utility, coupled with his ability to worry his way through to his goal.' In other words, the root of technology is creative ingenuity. Thus technology at its simplest (and I suspect at its most complicated) is concerned with solving other people's problems. It requires the clear statement of the problem, the consideration of alternatives and the elimination of the inappropriate, the following of a regular procedure, and some kind of quantitative assessment.

That is not to say that it is concerned *only* with the quantitative, still less only with the measurable, the calculable, the settled and the dead. Technology, as something involving innovation and change – creative ingenuity – demands an exercise of the imagination as much as of the intellect (if the two can be considered separately). There is no doubt, in the field of engineering, of the use of intuition as well as calculation – that is to say, not a wild emotional grasping at straws, but the use of a direct way of grasping the solution to a problem, not usually in one leap but as part of a continuing experience.

Technical education, in Whitehead's words, 'is creative experience while you think, experience which realises your thought, experience which teaches you to co-ordinate act and thought, experience leading you to associate thought with foresight and foresight with achievement. Technical education gives theory, and a shrewd insight as to where theory fails.' The engineers cited earlier are examples of this process; so are Felix Candela in our own time, and Paxton in landscaping. They are people characterized by a developed

and massive common sense based on experience, a very real
knowledge and the ability to envisage what was likely to
happen.

Here is a clear and simple statement of the process at
the most ordinary level — in the field of motor cycle
maintenance — from Pirsig's *Zen and the Art of Motorcycle
Maintenance*:

If you have to choose among an infinite number of ways
to put it together then the relation of the machine to you,
and the relation of the machine and you to the rest of the
world, has to be considered, because the selection from among
many choices, the *art* of the work is just as dependent upon
your own mind and spirit as it is upon the material of the
machine. That's why you need the peace of mind.... Some-
time look at a novice workman or a bad workman and compare
his expression with that of a craftsman whose work you
know is excellent and you'll see the difference. The craftsman
isn't following a single line of instruction. He's making
decisions as he goes along. For that reason he'll be absorbed
and attentive to what he's doing even though he doesn't
deliberately contrive this. His motions and the machine are
in a kind of harmony. He isn't following any set of written
instructions because the nature of the material at hand deter-
mines his thoughts and motions, which simultaneously change
the nature of the material at hand. The material and his
thoughts are changing together in a progression of changes
until his mind's at rest at the same time's the material's right.
'Sounds like art,' the instructor says.
'Well, it *is* art,' I say. 'This divorce of art from technology
is completely unnatural. It's just that it's gone on so long
you have to be an archaeologist to find out where the two
separated.'

Technik (to follow Fores' account in the *Higher Education Review*

Spring 1979, 'Technik: the relevance of a missing concept')
is

> the cultural area involved with the making, improving, main-
> taining, using and running of artefacts of the type which
> were once called 'contrivances' and which are very often
> machines of a sort. Among those with a higher education
> qualification the most important group of exponents of *Technik*
> are engineers ... the history of *Technik* shows that man has
> always used all the knowledge and ingenuity at his disposal
> to create useful artefacts. . . . Man's unique powers of foresight
> and imagination have been more directly useful to him through
> the exercise of *Technik,* rather than indirectly useful through
> building up a structured body of scientific knowledge ...
>
> *Technik* is a separate cultural area with codes of behaviour,
> responses and a dignity of its own.

Fores' views find powerful support in *Engineering our Future,*
the report of the Committee of Inquiry into the Engineering
Profession chaired by Sir Montague Finniston in 1980. In
referring to the tradition in the German *Technische Hochschule*
and French *Grandes Ecoles* based firmly upon the philosophy
and concept of *Technik* — the synthesis and practical
application of knowledge rather than those of scientific
scholarship — the Report comments that:

> This view of engineering science as an offshoot or application
> of science is held to have underlain many of the current
> criticisms of engineering formation in Britain today; in
> particular, *engineering courses constructed on the basis of teaching*
> first *the underlying scientific analysis and theory and* then *the*
> *potential applications of it, build into engineering formation a*
> *dichotomy between 'theory' and 'practice'.* This dichotomy does
> not arise in courses based upon the philosophy of 'Technik'
> which places everything taught firmly in the context of
> economic purpose. Theoretical teaching is from early on linked

to its potential usefulness within the overall theme of an engineering system, be it mechanical, electrical or process.

The final years of 'German model' and French engineering courses are then concentrated upon specialised projects designed to focus and bring together what had been learnt about various aspects of a particular system. The debate which has continually dogged engineering teachers over the appropriate balance in engineering formation between theory and practice is a non-issue within the continental mode of engineering teaching.

In relation to Britain's overseas competitors, the Report continues:

This deficiency to a large extent reflects the relatively restricted and narrow British conception of engineering as a branch of applied science, which militates against an effective marriage between theory and application. The British system does not give students sufficient grounding in the synthesis of technical, human and financial considerations nor does it adequately encourage the development of the wider skills and outlook required of engineers within the engineering dimension. In consequence employers have often taken the attitude that few engineers are properly equipped to take on broader managerial responsibilities and have employed them instead as providers of technical services.

The education and training of engineers needs a radical rethinking. The key to its extension lies not in more liberal studies, as we commonly insist, but in the focusing of the course on what the engineer actually does – that is, Design. Following the logic of its arguments, the Finniston Report emphasizes that,

Design practice should be a prominent and unifying theme of the course, (as is achieved in continental engineering formation)

and not an isolated expertise through the strong emphasis, particularly in the later years of their courses, on a specialised project which focuses the more general engineering theory and applications previously taught . . .

8 Design and Problem Solving

If we agree that we are, from beginning to end, concerned with finding things out and making things work, and that it is important that people should learn such skills and attitudes, then surely a key to educational progress must be to study the actual process of thinking out and making; that is, of *designing*. So I set out to see if, from the design process, we could abstract certain basic abilities or skills that could give the framework of a new kind of understanding — an education from the very start informed by action rather than inert knowledge. My contention is that design education, if taken seriously, could and would have a significant and creative influence on the entire educational system.

Let us look at the learning potential within a design task. There are, I believe, five identifiable stages in the sequence of designing and making:

Stage 1 is the identification, discovery and recognition of *NEEDS*, that is, finding out what the problem is, and what the designer has to do. That may sound simple, but it is in fact elusive. There is, for one thing, a considerable difference between what people think they need and what they may actually need: between what they want and what they need.

But even if that sounds paternalistic, the study of the technology of a particular area often throws up different realities from what was at first envisaged. The entire problem may need to be redefined. The identification of needs does not mean inventing needs unnecessarily or persuading people, as the consumer society relentlessly does, of new wants and creating a profusion of them; it means identifying genuine needs, which may mean dispensing with some and discovering the real ones.

Stage 2 is the collection of information, the assembly of *FACTS*. That is fairly straightforward, ranging from everything known about the artefact or similar artefacts, to the techniques and technology appropriate to the problem. This is to a large extent an exercise in history — the history of the identifiable immediate past.

Stage 3 in my sequence comes the *ANALYSIS* of those needs and facts — the drawn-out, difficult and totally demanding intellectual exercise of putting all the aspects together, eliminating the irrelevant or unworkable, thinking out alternatives and reaching an understanding of what the problem really is. This is the stage that calls for what educational theorists are now recognizing the need for, without which no progress is possible — analytical thought. It is a power which anyone in an industrial and urban society needs: possibly the most difficult to develop in the individual. Anyone who has known or worked with a person with a power of that kind, as I have done, knows its presence and its effect; it cuts through the fog of words and illusions like a cold keen wind. It includes the moment, or the extended time, when the mind (its reason and imagination) grapples with the whole of the problem, its demands and its possible means, comes to terms with them, discards, selects, tests, rejects, draws, makes experiments, thinks, and thinks again; and sometimes after a period of agony emerges from the dark with an idea.

Stage 4 is that *IDEA*. In most fields of design, an idea, whether it is for a building or an artefact or a machine or a process, may be a kind of transparent image or it may be a piece of logic; but essentially it is a unity — it is the new potential thing which exists or will exist to bring together and make into one the needs and techniques, the demands and the means. It is a totality. And it is the moment in the making of a thing when it potentially has a name to describe and define the new totality. From that moment it can never really cease to exist.

Stage 5 is *REALIZATION*, which is self-explanatory, except to indicate that I mean the first realization of the idea, the point at which a lot of disadvantages may appear, as the thing takes shape and works or fails to work for the first time. If it fails or is seriously impaired, it may drive you back to further thought and analysis, and may involve the discarding of the idea and the formulation of a new one. It is followed by *IMPLEMENTATION* which is again self-explanatory except that it involves production, and often repetition: always the work and energy of other people.

I do not pretend that that sequence contains a complete key to education in the world of work. Rather, I outline it because there are certain features worth comment in that process, which is in fact a more common activity than conventional learning processes. For instance, it does not follow the usual sequence of rational thought — thesis, antithesis, synthesis; or proposition, opposition, solution — which are taken for granted in our accepted procedures of learning and thinking in debate. Since my sequence may not be adequate in all instances — for example, to describe the thinking that goes into innovation in engineering design — I outline below a more sophisticated approach, for which I am indebted to a paper by Douglas Lewin of Brunel University. This approach is associated with a systems approach to engineering. In that the starting point is the problem; and since that is in any case the starting-point for technology or any technological exercise it is convenient to start there as well. In such a case the key to the start of the process is *specification of the problem*. It is followed, not later, as I suggested above, but immediately by a creative stage in which the designer tries out a solution. It may not amount to much, but it does help to correct any false assumption and establish that it is possible to find a solution of some sort. This is followed by the analysis of the idea once it is known to be feasible.

The point to note is that this is exactly the opposite from the process if the study were one in applied science. The traditional scientific method is that of *induction*, still used despite Hume's exposition of its inherent fault in the eighteenth century. In the inductive method enough observations are made to derive from them a general law; if enough experiments are made it may be possible to validate the hypothesis. The problem with induction, as Hume pointed out, is that it is impossible to prove that there is no exception to the general rule. It only needs one to invalidate the whole: the scientist can never be absolutely certain that there is no possible exception and that future events will always obey laws that were based on past observations.

Popper, to whom I have already referred in connection with World 3 and the problem of dualism, destroys the theory of induction – or rather bypasses it by rejecting the usual scientific method. His thesis is simple. While it is impossible to prove a statement and validate it beyond doubt, it is possible to prove its falsification; it only requires one observation to disprove a general theory. All scientific progress therefore follows from the disproving of assumptions as a continuous process until a theory much nearer the truth emerges. It is the reverse of the traditional inductive process. Instead of proceeding from observations to theory, the scientist proceeds from theory to observations. The process begins with the *formulation of a problem*, proceeds to some *proposed solution*, and thence to the deduction of testable propositions, to experimental tests and to the evaluation of competing theories. In other words, it moves from postulating the solution to a problem to tests that may prove its falsification. The formulation of the problem is crucial.

Popper's own formulation of the process, which he sees as one of continuous development, is as follows:

$$P1 \rightarrow TS \rightarrow EE \rightarrow P2$$

where P1 is the initial problem, TS is a trial solution, EE is error elimination and P2 the restatement of the problem. Clearly, the process is indefinite. There can never be a final solution, only one getting closer to the truth. And that, of course, is exactly the case for anything in the field of design and making. There is never a unique solution in anything to do with design or engineering, and the one adopted may not even be the most efficient, for a number of reasons. The attraction of the Popperian sequence is precisely that it bears more relation to the real world of man-made things than to the artificial world in which there are thought to be correct solutions.

But you would not think so to judge from what we are doing in the educational world today. It seems extraordinarily difficult to escape from the conventional way of looking at things. For example, in an admirable report by the British Association for the Advancement of Science in 1977, the authors cannot in the end escape from the conventions of education, however radical they think their recommendations are. When it comes to the training of the professional engineer, they comment on the 'international agreement' that a combined process of education and training is essential to the development of a professional engineer. It may be analysed, in broad terms, into three stages:

(a)   education in the principles of engineering science;
(b)   education/training in the application of these principles to the analysis and solution of engineering problems;
(c)   objective training, related to the particular requirements of the engineer's first substantive appointment.

That sequence must have seemed to them so natural as to be beyond question or criticism. In fact it is an orthodox, conventional, easy-to-organize, easy-to-rationalize, pedagogical procedure that combines satisfaction for the teacher with utter boredom for the pupil. *In human experience the principles* (if there are any) *are subsequent to the discovery and solution of problems.* But it is easier to plan courses and teach the other way round.

Let me contrast that with a more colourful reference. In an outstanding chapter in Singer's *History of Technology*, Sir Eric Ashby quoted some fascinating evidence on the education of boys given to the Select Committee on Scientific Instruction in 1868 by Sir Joseph Whitworth:

First of all I would give notice that there would be competition of half-a-dozen boys in the use of the knife, and I would have a carpenter prepare half-a-dozen cylindrical pieces of wood eight inches long, and one inch in diameter, and I would ask those boys to make it square by the use of the knife. In the first trial I would have a piece of white deal . . . On the second trial I would have a red deal, and on the third trial, beech, or ash, or oak. That would be teaching those little boys the different natures of woods, at the same time that they would be learning to sharpen the knife according to the wood they would be operating upon. You would want a very different edge for oak and for white deal. Then, if you found a boy with a very good intellect he might, perhaps, be a surgeon, while a boy with less brain might be a butcher or a shoemaker; but this knowledge of the use of the knife must do good to all of them.

Here, comments Ashby, *is the quintessence of technical education.* I agree with him. How unfortunate that no one seems to have taken the slightest notice. Experience of teaching in this field confirms for many of us that *the real task in the teaching of skills is to teach them so well and so thoroughly that it becomes possible to abstract from them general principles that can then be used and applied in a new situation.*

Not only the principles, but the skills themselves. Skills are fundamental, even in our changing technological world; they are the guarantees of competence. It will not do to teach only the principles, as if they were unchanging. There is among educational theorists a common assumption that if we make sure that we do not know how to do any single thing properly we shall be in a strong position to change from one job to another. It is an illusion. In a world of uncertainty and change, how to do something well is a better basis for moving to cope with the unknown than a wide liberal and general education. Since Edward de Bono first popularized theories of lateral thinking, much more has been found about the right hemisphere of the brain (the side which governs special awareness and creativity); yet these findings have had only a limited effect on education. We remain content to let that side of the brain moulder, and continue to concentrate on the hard-edged, numerical and verbal skills which form the basis of university disciplines and our exam-ridden liberal education. We are not even fully ready to admit that activities like design are supremely educative, in that they draw on the capabilities of *both* sides of the brain.

So where can such a process of design be experienced? Not in our universities, which shy away from elusive or ambiguous activities and take shelter in disciplines or subjects for their own sake (which are easy to examine and where the quality of work is easy to assess through the production of learned papers). Nor in those colleges which, seeking status, ape university patterns. One of the turning points for me in relation to this matter occurred a few years ago when, after studying the work of the teacher training colleges, it struck me that quite a few subjects only existed because they were taught. If they weren't taught at all, I suddenly realized, they wouldn't need to exist. I hurried to consult a most eminent educator whose views and work I profoundly respect. He was surprised that I should only just have discovered this fact. I am still reeling at the thought of teaching nothing because it makes an impressive-looking syllabus. Of course it also provides teaching jobs.

The places where the design process can be experienced as part of learning are, with varying degrees of success, in one of the areas which our educational hierarchy consigns to the lower level than the universities. That is, in the Schools of Art and Design, where in everything from Fine Art to Industrial Design, the sequence for the stimulation of creative ingenuity is followed − or should be. And of course, in the polytechnics − or should be. For the challenge that has been before them since their creation is to achieve standards of learning equal to those achieved in the universities, but through a process of thought based upon the analysis of problems and the exercise of creative ingenuity.

If we use this culture of doing and making as a guide to the development of an education, it must be the case that it leads to a system of learning very different from the traditional one. It can become a cycle, a more appropriate cycle than the usual deadly round of academic disciplines, taught and learned from school to college to university to school again. It must be characterized by the fact that things happen, that new things are made, that new recognitions of nature are achieved, that things work or do not work. It must be an education based upon doing something, not passively receiving it but, as *homo faber*, worrying one's way through to the goal. It involves intuition as well as rationalization and the development of an acute perception in the active understanding of things. If its starting-point is activity, its great moment is discovery and its reward is freedom – the freedom to do and know and change and invent, the freedom that arises from the competence to do something as opposed to the slavery of not being able to do it and therefore having to make do with something else.

It has other fundamental characteristics. For instance, it follows a process, rationally and critically, which must be completed in order to make sense at all and cannot be left off after study of the difficulties (in the respectable academic way of: on the one hand, ... and on the other ...). Furthermore, its end is a product or an activity, not a question, a challenge or a theory. In the world of things a thing has to exist. In that sense the world is not the same as it was before. It is now occupied by a new thing. Above all, it demands cooperation, the ability to work with other people. Nothing can either be found out in the way of needs or realized and implemented without working as a group or a team. And that is an essential lesson for working in the real world. It follows that this kind of education is not, as traditional education is, the province of the isolated individual, the privileged or the academic. It is an education through what we anyway do, for Everyman. It is precisely what this country needs.

Design, to sum up, is an aspect of problem-solving – the working-out of a solution to a stated problem either by the use of available techniques or by the invention of new ones. It is fitting an answer to a problem in one, two, three or four dimensions, or the redefining of the problem and the discovery of an appropriate way of solving it. Design and invention are crucially related. In the words of Ruskin, *design, properly so-called,* is *human invention consulting human capacity.* And this leads to the consideration of some of the factors which must ultimately affect any relevant education. In the field of design, of problems, of invention, especially human problems, you never have exact statements. You never, for example, have all the necessary information upon which to base your design, and of what you have much is probably wrong anyway.

But to give such a problem to students in an educational system strikes at its very roots. Academics like to have exact problems if only so that there will be exact answers; that makes it easier to mark papers. And since both academics and students are obsessed with examinations (the passing of which is the only problem they have considered) design is unpopular. In any design task there is always more than one answer to the problem; and there may indeed, be no completely satisfactory answer to it anyway. Furthermore, all design problems are continuous. There is never a final answer (look only at the motor car industry), so you cannot easily bring things to a halt. In that context if you look at the capacities that a good student ought to have they may well include the capacity to deal with the problem: What do you do when things go wrong?

I believe that one of the functions of higher education is to learn to tolerate uncertainty. If we presume we are trying to educate for life, perhaps another is to learn to take action from that position, for these are two capabilities that will be constantly demanded of our adult citizens in the world of today.

9 Action: The Basis for a New Theory of Education

There are two very natural propensities which we may distinguish in the most virtuous and liberal dispositions, the love of pleasure and the love of action. If the former is refined by art and learning, improved by the charms of social intercourse, and corrected by a just regard to economy, to health, and to reputation, it is productive of the greatest part of the happiness of private life. The love of action is a principle of a much stronger and more doubtful nature. It often leads to anger, to ambition, and to revenge; but when it is guided by the sense of propriety and benevolence, it becomes the parent of every virtue, and, if those virtues are accompanied with equal abilities, a family, a state, or an empire may be indebted for their safety and prosperity to the undoubted courage of a single man. To the love of pleasure we may therefore ascribe most of the agreeable, to the love of action we may attribute most of the useful and respectable, qualifications. The character in which both the one and the other should be united and harmonised would seem to constitute the most perfect idea of human nature.

That was written in the eighteenth century by Edward Gibbon

in *The Decline and Fall of the Roman Empire*, chapter 15, where he discusses the progress of Christianity. It will serve as an appropriate introduction to the attempt to find a new and more comprehensive kind of education. It is also ironic, because if Gibbon thought it possible in his time that such a perfect idea of human nature could be realized, the intellectual movements of his century and especially the next were making such a happening increasingly unlikely.

It was as if the structure of western society had been specially shaped to emphasize the conflict between thought and action. The bifurcation of higher education in the nineteenth century was however not just the result of a pragmatic solution to a practical situation; it rested, I believe, upon a deeper characteristic in Western European thought. That is the dualism that has characterized so much of our thinking since the Enlightenment.

There is, of course, considerable justification in nature for thinking in dualistic terms, starting with the human body: duplication of the organs, the fact that we have two sexes ... We also tend to think in poles — positive and negative poles — and the binary system. In the western world even our aesthetic senses insist on dualism and balance. I got quite a shock, coming from the tradition of balanced sentences, vases at either end of the mantelpiece, classical pillars on either side of the front door, to find, on entering a mosque in Turkey, that the caliph's kiosk may jut out into the central space at any angle and from any point in the wall; that blue tiles change their pattern as you go round the walls apparently wherever they run out of their supply of a particular pattern. In Europe, where a style lacks dualism and balance, like the Rococo, it is considered highly and distinctively *outré*. Yet a Japanese flower or garden arrangement has no such severe mental rules to obey.

The dualism of much of our philosophy is often related

to the philosophy of Kant, but it is really much more generalized than that and has become typical of our day-to-day thinking, as well as being an inheritance from nineteenth-century Platonism. There is the obvious dualism of theory and practice, but there are other aspects – mind and body, mind and matter, appearance and reality, subjective and objective, etc. It has almost become a common habit of thought that we investigate an apparently confused problem, sort it out into two mutually antipathetic alternatives and resolve a decision in favour of one or the other.(To this our parliamentary system and the layout of Parliament may contribute. It is a consoling thought that every problem can be reduced to two alternatives and that political parties will sooner or later adopt one or the other. It is becoming a little less clear now that that convention can be sustained indefinitely.) The dualism with which I am concerned in this chapter is that between thought and action. To quote Whitehead again,

> An evil side of the Platonic culture has been its total neglect of technical education as an ingredient in the complete development of ideal human beings. This neglect has arisen from two disastrous antitheses, namely, that between mind and body, and that between thought and action.

In two thought-provoking books by John MacMurray, the former Professor of Moral Philosophy in the University of Edinburgh, this problem is exhaustively discussed (John MacMurray, *The Self as Agent* and *Persons in Relation*). MacMurray makes the point that many of these dualisms are unreal. For example the mind/body problem is, in fact, 'no problem but a patent absurdity'. (We can all cite instances of our medical advisers getting tied in knots by adhering to their idea of human beings as a dualistic mind/body problem.) In the face of our problems – for example, our commitment to a planned society in which planning must involve the unity of theory and practice — it is essential to eliminate the traditional dualism and look at experience as a whole. 'The unity of experience as a whole,' he writes, 'is not a unity of knowledge, but a unity of personal activities of which knowledge is only one.' Where does he find that unity? He finds it in *action*, for action 'is a unity of knowledge and movement'. He rejects dualism 'through asserting the primacy of the practical'. For *'it is the practical that is primary; the theoretical is secondary and derivative.'* That is surely a reversal of what we usually assume. There are good reasons for MacMurray's contention:

> In thinking the mind alone is active. In acting the body indeed is active, but also the mind. Action is not blind. *When we turn from reflection to action we do not turn from consciousness to unconsciousness.* When we act, sense, perception and judgement are in continuous activity, along with physical movement'.

MacMurray's thesis seems to me directly relevant to the changes in education with which I am concerned. It is not just that throughout the history of education, and specifically during the nineteenth century, the gap widened between thought and action; it seems to have led to the belief that thought was in some way superior and action an inferior part of the whole. In terms of education this meant — and I believe that education still has this belief, however subconsciously — that the highest levels of education were concerned with thought or reflection for its own sake, and that any kind of activity was in some way a travesty of that purity. Knowledge for its own sake was, as nineteenth-century Oxford indicated, the highest peak to which an education could aspire.

It is fundamental to the new synthesis that I am attempting to reach that action — not for its own sake but as part of, and indeed the completion of, thought — is in every way as estimable, and may even be more so. It follows that there must be some implication for the individual or individuals involved in action as well as in or including thought. To quote MacMurray again: 'The starting-point of personal development, since a person is an agent, is the development of the ability to act.' But as soon as one says that action is the very basis of personal development, it must be the case that the starting-point for reflection and for study is no longer the individual by himself (who has always seemed the starting-point for a philosophy) but a number of individuals in relationship to each other. To quote MacMurray again: 'The isolated, purely individual self is a fiction in philosophy. This means, as we shall see, that the unity of the personal cannot be thought as the form of an individual self, but only through the mutuality of personal relationship.'

Now, in my own words, the basic unit for our kind of society is not the individual person or the individual student, it is someone in relation to something or someone else. That is what is involved in action. *There is no such thing as action in isolation. Action involves the reaction or interaction of someone else.* Or to summarize, the dualism of thought and action is a nonsense; the unity of experience requires action; action involves more than one person in isolation; but paradoxically, it is the key to personal development.

What are the implications of this?

First, I think it means that the starting-point for our educational planning, both as regards courses and disciplines, requires rethinking in terms of *groups* of people, the relationships between them and between them and the studies involved. For example, *the measure of success should not in*

principle be merely that someone has acquired so much knowledge;
it should be that someone has acquired the skill to do something
effectively with it.

Secondly, it means that *our systems of promotion and staff*
development should be based, not just upon scholarship and learning,
but upon the ability to carry out tasks — in this case, primarily
the task of teaching. That, of course, at the level of higher
education, is not as simple as it sounds. Teaching at this
level cannot be satisfactorily performed without constant
study and investigation. But the study is not the end in
itself; it is a means towards the more complete performance
of teaching.

Thirdly, there are implications for the kind of studies
involved. The very nature of knowledge itself is affected
by the use to which it is to be put and the modes of thinking
which encompass it. I suspect that facts, or what pass for
facts, are actually different when they are seen in a context
of action and not in a context of reflection. For action involves
the recognition of *things* as such. To quote Whitehead: 'There
is no substitute for the direct perception of the concrete
achievement of a thing in its actuality.' Without that kind
of perception it is not possible to *do* anything.

It follows, I believe, from the implications I have outlined,
that the sources of material for our education, the generators
of our total experience, are not simply words and certainly
not just books. They are, so to speak, 'out there'. In that
sense, the centre of a useful education is not really the library.
The library is an essential tool; but there are many others.
They include the facts, the lives, the other people — in short,
real life.

Real life is never as neat as the scholar's summary in his
book. In real life one can never get all the information, and
much of what he gets is contradictory. This is why simple

answers to complex questions are not very educational. The point is that young people must be educated to look for data outside books so that they will be better able to handle the world outside academia. The professors in our universities too often try to make students into carbon copies of themselves.

That remark comes from a thought-provoking paper by the Director of the East–West Center at Honolulu, Mr Everett Kleinjans. For him, in the new situation we are trying to develop, the student must begin

to look for data out in the reality of society and not just in his professor's lectures, the library, or the laboratory. In fact, the street, the town, the field become his primary sources. He learns to deal with the knowledge of everyday life. His task is to figure out how to make order out of complexity or chaos.

And that involves a new look at the nature of knowledge. He quotes Drucker (*The Age of Discontinuity*, 1969):

For the intellectual, knowledge is what is in a book. But *as long as it is in the book, it is only 'information' if not mere 'data'. Only when a man applies the information to do something does it become knowledge. Knowledge, like electricity or money, is a form of energy that exists only when doing work.*

It must be the case that such knowledge cannot be acquired in isolation or privacy; it requires cooperation. And that is true of society as a whole. It may well be the case that a study in depth can be carried through in isolation. The *application* of that study undoubtedly demands collaboration – the joint pursuit of what Whitehead called 'the art of the utilization of knowledge'. For that, after all, is what we need. To return to Kleinjans again:

The world does not really need more humanistic ideas or

loftier ideals. But it *does* need people who have the desire and the talent to devise ways of translating good ideas or high ideals into workable schemes for ordinary human beings. This challenge implies the necessity to concern ourselves with the common knowledge of everyday life and to develop the skills of problem solving, decision making, and managing. We should attempt to develop solution-oriented people.

His conclusion is one which seems more natural to me with every year: 'Education which has not trained men to see ambiguity, to make decisions, and to accept responsibility for their decisions, has not equipped them for life in modern society.'

If the task I have outlined is the right one, there cannot be one place or one kind of institution of higher education that can carry it out precisely. The more action-oriented all institutions become, the more demand there is for such courses from potential students and from society, the more varied and complex should *all* the institutions be. At the end of the day, the institutions may overlap and may seem identical — but only in the sense that organisms of varied and multiple kinds resemble each other in that parts of them may be identical.

Now let me take the implications a little further. I argued earlier in this book that the key to the educational ethos of the country lies in the universities. There is, I am sure, no escaping that. It is what parents and teachers aim for; it is what attracts the media; it is what influences governments, the professions and society as a whole. What was disastrous in the Robbins Report, which established the principles on which higher education was expanded, was not the emphasis on the universities, *but the belief inherent in it that if higher education were to be available to everyone it should be of the same kind as when it applied only to an elite.* We have accepted the need of education for all but have failed to re-examine its content.

I also argued earlier that the universities have a powerful ethos developed in the last 150 years at the centre of which is the ideal of a liberal education. So powerful is it that it affects all the institutions welcomed into the groves of academe — colleges of advanced technology, new universities, colleges dependent upon university degrees.

It might, of course, be argued that the universities should do something to change those attitudes. It would be difficult; the ethos is very well established. But in any case, it is surely crucial that the universities should not be in any way weakened; if anything, they should be strengthened in their independence. Perhaps there should be fewer of them and better ones. Another alternative, advocated at one time by the editor of the *Times Higher Educational Supplement*, is that the only way to solve the problem is to extend the university system. There are between 70 and 80 major institutions, including the universities and polytechnics. We might call them all universities and thus broaden the idea of the university. It would certainly have some advantages. Most of the present polytechnics labour under the serious disadvantage of a shortage of non-academic staff and niggling interference in their day-to-day affairs by the local authorities who have no concept of their work. But widening the scope of the universities may not solve the problem I have been outlining. As I emphasized above, *we need greater variety — high standards with different curricula rather than uniform curricula with different standards*. We need more change, more freedom. We will probably have more freedom if there is better control at the centre, by the government.

But education as a whole must be genuinely comprehensive. The polytechnics are part of that world, at the level of tertiary education. They suffer from all sorts of disadvantages —

probably less the lack of money than the chaotic apparatus of controls over them and their own consequent management. If the government is committed to the future prosperity of this country, it must give some priority to the institutions which struggle to work towards that prosperity against every obstacle.

That is a comment about some of the institutions; but we must look further for an answer to our problem. For the world of human endeavour, what kind of mind, what abilities are needed? To start with, it is necessary to put things in the right order. We would all, I imagine, agree that literacy and numeracy are crucial in our society. But it is easy to think of them as ends in themselves. They are not ends but only means to something else – to understanding and to action. They are necessary but not sufficient. We need at least a third means or ability which has a direct bearing upon the modern world, that has to do with visual awareness or acuity – the ability to perceive and understand in three dimensions. It is necessary for the understanding of many subjects, like advanced mathematics; it is essential for production work, for design of all kinds. And design is the one underrated activity which is central to every single technological and environmental development happening in front of our eyes. It is not art in the sense of aesthetics; it is not whimsy; it is not an expression of conventional taste; it is the thinking out of objects and machines which affect our lives. And whether or not people are trained specifically in design, design is being carried out all the time.

So we come back to it. What do we need?

If to these three attributes – literacy, numeracy and spatial awareness – we add manual skill, the world of learning takes on a different shape. For manual skill as I understand it is not just a description of a physical event but of an activity which involves the mind and body and also requires will-power. Skills if applied at the level which our advanced society demands cannot be discussed in terms of the traditional dualism of mind and body. There is much more involved. It must include decision making and the carrying out of decisions, whether our own or those of others. Addressing a conference on Higher Education in Newcastle in 1976 (*Higher Education: For what and for whom?*), Sir Toby Weaver put it this way:

> I am thinking of a person's general capacity to manage his own life, to cope with his environment, to profit from experience, to master what used to be called the art of living, to reach sensible decisions and act on them. To call this quality gumption or *nous* is to incur the charge of vulgarity; to call it wisdom verges on the high faluting; to call it lifemanship lacks seriousness. May I settle for CAPABILITY as the nearest I can get to describing the ability to apply one's stock of knowledge and manifold of skills, as Bacon put it, for the benefit and use of man.

In 1977 a small group of academics, industrialists and civil servants met at the London Business School to discuss the Crisis in Education and ask whether there was any way to find a new direction for it. All of them had in one way or another been writing or lecturing about the crisis, covering much of the material and views expressed in this book (but by no means necessarily agreeing with them all). They met under the provisional title *Homo Faber* and ended by formulating a statement under the title *Education for Capability*, the statement printed at the start of this book;

> We believe that there is a serious imbalance in Britain today in the full process which is described by the two words 'education' and 'training'. Thus, the idea of the 'educated man' is that of a scholarly, leisured individual who has been neither educated nor trained to exercise useful skills. Those who study

in secondary schools or higher education increasingly specialise; and normally in a way which means that they are taught to practise only the skills of scholarship and science; to understand but not to act. They gain knowledge of a particular area of study, but not ways of thinking and working which are appropriate for use outside the education system.

We believe that this imbalance is harmful to individuals, to industry and to society. Individual satisfaction stems from doing a job well through the exercise of personal capability. Acquisition of this capability is inhibited by the present system of education which stresses the importance of analysis, criticism and the acquisition of knowledge and generally neglects the formulation and solution of problems, doing, making and organising; in fact, constructive and creative activity of all sorts.

The resolution of this problem in Britain has been vitiated by discussing it in terms of two cultures: the arts and the sciences. It is significant that we have no word for the culture that the Germans describe as 'Technik' or the mode of working that the French describe as a 'metier'.

We consider that there exists in its own right a culture which is concerned with doing, making and organising. This culture emphasises craftsmanship and the making of useful artefacts; the design, manufacture and marketing of goods and services; specialist occupations with an active mode of work; the creative arts; and the day to day management of affairs.

We believe that education should spend more time in teaching people skills and preparing them for life outside the education system; and that the country would benefit significantly in economic terms from this re-balancing towards education for capability.

The statement was signed by many public figures and published in *The Times* and *The Guardian*; the handling of the movement's affairs was undertaken by the Royal Society of Arts, established in the eighteenth century for 'the Encouragement of Arts Manufactures and Commerce'.

It should be noted that Capability does not mean a revolution but simply a change of direction, a righting of the imbalance of our educational world. For an emphasis on doing does not mean the rejection of thinking. As I have already pointed out, any serious kind of doing and making involves thinking as well. But it does suggest a change in the way education is divided and subdivided, into subjects and disciplines. If we are serious about education for the world of work, we must deal with activities rather than subjects, with courses rather than disciplines; we need a radical regrouping of knowledge and action. The subjects should not be ends in themselves as they are at the moment; they should be means to an end — understanding and action, work and satisfaction. Such a regrouping is encountered in practice. As soon as you try to apply advanced knowledge or research to practical affairs, you have to cross academic boundaries and break down the barriers of conventional disciplines. It follows that an education based on the idea of Capability ought, in principle, to enable people to escape the status problems inherent in the present system. It is a matter of experience in work of many kinds that status problems begin to disappear when you are deeply involved in trying to do something together. Status matters a great deal to people of leisure, who have plenty of time to reflect on it, and need a device to keep people at a distance and protect themselves. In the activity of working together there is no reason to believe that everyone must be paid the same or do the same job; experience tells us that people have different responsibilities, different abilities and skills; there is nothing unusual in a good craftsman's recognizing that another craftsman has different and perhaps greater skills than he has. Mutual respect stems from action not from inaction; nothing replaces the respect for someone who knows how to do his or her job well and gets on with it. *Status ceases to be a problem when people are working well together.*

A further implication of 'Education for Capability' was outlined by Tyrrell Burgess in his lecture to the Royal Society of Arts, *New Ways to Learn* (1978). He distinguished between two basic traditions in education: the autonomous and the service tradition. The autonomous tradition is the one enshrined by the universities and discussed already in this book; the service tradition centres upon service to society. Service to society does not mean following its obvious conventions. Service to society, especially by an educational institution, includes critizing it. That is one of the important functions of a university. The difficulty is to make serious and constructive criticism if one does not know enough about it.

Burgess has elaborated upon that distinction by coining the phrase 'academic drift' to identify the trend which seems inevitable whereby institutions in the service sector gradually become institutions in the autonomous sector. There are plenty of examples. Secondary schools, given a chance, become grammar schools; polytechnics often want to be universities. Burgess also points out that *the vocational nature of a course depends less upon its subject-matter than upon its method.* I think this is important. You can teach skills in many ways; at the most basic level you can either teach people to practise the skill itself, or you can teach them to describe it and appreciate it. The challenge to the service sector is to *practise* the skills.

Let me try to follow the logic of this argument and see where it leads in terms of actual proposals. We have looked at the nature of technology and design and seen that technology is what creates the environment of today and enables man to control it; we have also seen that in that environment almost everything is designed by someone. We have gone on to outline the idea of capability, and suggest that pupils of all types and abilities might be educated in the culture of doing and making and organizing. We have seen that this is not a narrow world but one much wider and more exciting than the world of books and blackboards.

Any education that starts with technology and design must start with activities, with doing and making. The key is in the definition of problems; the activity is problem-solving. But it is not enough to solve problems intellectually; it is necessary to implement decisions. Many people can make decisions; the difficulty is implementing them.

Are there certain basic abilities or skills that everyone ought to have? If there is to be a genuinely comprehensive education, suitable for all, and if at least up to a certain age every boy and girl should follow the course, can we identify certain basic abilities? Are there certain generic skills which everyone should learn, which will be available in any occupation, however unforeseen? Or are there transferable skills — that is, skills themselves based upon trained capacities which enable someone to teach him- or herself a new skill without dismay — which should form part of a National Curriculum?

What is quite clear to me is that any relevant education must start with the everyday, the experience of the close at hand, the understanding of ordinary things. It follows from that that the process should not move from general rules or generalities to applications, but from the understanding of the particular — an event, an artefact or a natural object — from which it should be possible to generalize and formulate a rule or a concept.

But knowledge of the particular is a different kind of knowledge from knowledge of the general. It requires not just the use of discursive reasoning but the direct apprehension of the thing in its actuality. The direct way of grasping a reality based upon experience is sometimes called intuition – that is, knowledge of the individual thing.

The implications of this are various and formidable. It means that the kind of knowledge I am talking about cannot just be handed on by a body of scholars. If it could, it would not be the kind of knowledge I am seeking. The only way that kind of knowledge can be obtained is by discovering it for yourself. Each pupil has to find out individually, not by learning from a book but from the apprehension of the thing in its totality. 'First-hand knowledge', said Whitehead, 'is the ultimate basis of intellectual life.'

How does this happen? It requires help and practice. I do not know anyone who has acquired the habit of learning the real and the actual without being guided by another person who shares in the wonder of discovery. The thrill of learning happens when the student personally makes a connection between things and discovers a reality greater than he could otherwise have imagined. To do that a student needs to be aided and challenged and guided. But equally crucial is the fact that that kind of knowledge cannot be acquired by the ordinary process of studying subjects and disciplines. The key to it is experience, and experience requires guidance.

What is this experience? It is experience of the familiar now understood in a new light and a greater totality. That is done not just by reasoning or rote, it requires insights. The grasp of reality is ultimately an artistic experience.

I want to finish this chapter with a personal comment. We, the children of the industrial and social revolutions, are no longer concerned exclusively with an intellectual elite; we are concerned with learning for Everyman – learning to some purpose. It may be painful for some; it must be right for all. For we are already producing in Britain twice as many graduates as there are jobs which traditionally graduates used to expect to have. They will have to adjust. So must the educators and the politicians.

The irony is that over the last century *we have developed an educational system that rewards and elevates precisely those people who can least contribute to society.* Imprisoned in their disciplines, narrowed into their specialisms, we train them with the utmost rigour to be unable to cope with the real, immediate world. But, as we increasingly find, any real problems and any innovation demand that we cross those boundaries and work together. As soon as advanced knowledge is applied to the real world, the boundaries of the disciplines become a barrier to progress. Tinkering with the educational system is not enough. We have had plenty of reorganization, usually of the structure rather than of the realities of teaching. Reorganization does not solve everything; it merely enables academics and administrators to achieve their dream of sitting for ever on committees, with the illusion of power and the reality of idleness. What we need is much more basic — ultimately, I suppose, a change of heart, in which we rediscover the wonder of the world and of the ordinary, the magic of everyday. That is not a call for the prosaic. Far from it. It demands a love of the unexpected. It needs a certain idealism. It is a call not to be terrified of the unexpected, of change, of technological progress and development, but to go out to all these things, to teach pupils and students of the exciting potential of our world — there for Man to work through and with and upon, alongside others, as the Bible has it, to 'renew the face of the earth'.

10 Schools

Since I started working on the ideas which form the heart of this book, there are signs that a new movement towards the capability approach is gaining ground in educational circles. The most formal indication of this comes with the new school-leaving examinations, introduced by Sir Keith Joseph when he was Secretary for Education and Science. Scotland led the way with the Scottish Certificate of Education, Standard Grade, and England and Wales followed with the General Certificate of Secondary Education. The purpose of both is to provide one examination to be taken at 16 (school-leaving age) by all pupils of whatever standard. In addition, the new syllabuses are wide enough for each school to choose the form it considers most appropriate, and incorporate both the possibility of moving away from the theoretical to the practical and of more active learning and problem-solving.

It would be very good to think we had got there. But almost before the venture was launched, critical voices were raised. These were not only voices from the embattled establishment, who like the system tightly buttoned up into the discipline-divided and examinable compartments they are used to dealing with. But others, welcoming change, feel that the very width of choice allows the status quo to be maintained (and, of course, this is much easier than the

introduction of new syllabuses, new methods, and new ways
of testing attainments) and feel that the grading of pupils
in advance to decide who will take which form of exam
and at what level, may mean that no real change is achieved.
Will it just prove more of the same? Are we really going
to cross the divide between theory and practice, obliterating
it and see learning that prepares pupils for the world of
work as moving without distinction between the two? How
are we going to translate attainments of all sorts into
examinable situations? No wonder people are doubtful, for
it is a monstrous and monolithic system that the changes
in teaching and examinations are opposing. Can we affect
a true transformation while the examination boards remain
tied to the universities? Will a National Curriculum
encompass both theory and practice, satisfy basic needs
and open up possibilities for pupils of every type and range
of ability?

It is not only the teachers but the general public, and
particularly parents, who exert pressure to retain the old
pattern. The independent schools — and especially the public
schools — have usually been quite explicit about this. Why
do parents spend money sending their child to a public school?
They do so because that way they are more likely to get
into a university. Since the public schools' record of getting
their pupils into universities is noticeably better than that of
the majority of state schools, parents ambitious for the future
of their children will at least consider (and sometimes at great
sacrifice spend the money) sending them to an independent
school. Their path to university is straighter and less cluttered
by obstacles. It is assumed that the school work will be intelli-
gently planned so that entry to a university is the likely outcome. But not just any university: the public schools are geared
to the universities of Oxford and Cambridge. A measure of
that is the fact that, with only a handful of exceptions, the

headmasters who are members of the Headmasters Conference – membership of which defines a school as being a public school – are graduates of Oxford or Cambridge. Some of them have been (and will be again) tutors or masters of colleges. The continuity between the public schools and Oxford and Cambridge is obvious and deliberate. As the able headmaster of one of the leading public schools said to me, 'I am not paid to get boys into a polytechnic; nor am I paid to get them into any university. I am paid to get them into a good university, and preferably Oxford or Cambridge. And I do a jolly good job.'

While that remains the clear aim of the parents and the manifest expertise of the people providing the schooling at some of the most successful and prestigious schools in the country, it is interesting but unhelpful to talk about abolishing the system. But it is worth enquiring what constitutes a good school and a successful school career. If we assume that the best universities are Oxford and Cambridge, and if we assume that the best schools are those which can get their pupils into those universities, there is no real advantage in complaining about their prestige. This is the reality and it might as well be accepted that the best way to improve on the present is to build on what is there. It would also be a mistake to assume that Oxford and Cambridge teach only a certain kind of subject, that they are restricted to the useless arts and the pure sciences. Medicine had, of course, been part of their programme from the earliest days, although they took a long time to introduce it compared with their continental counterparts. Both had, by the end of the nineteenth or the early years of the twentieth century set up schools of engineering. There were in any case, and especially in Cambridge, centres of excellence renowned for their work and teaching in mathematics. So the school curricula devised to get pupils into the ancient universities could be varied and diverse and not restricted to the obvious needs of the school-leaving examinations.

The problem of the public schools is not in themselves but in the fact that the state schools emulate them. If it is the declared aim of the public schools to get their pupils into Oxford and Cambridge, it is the less explicit but no less demanding aim of the comprehensive schools to do the same — to get *some* of their pupils into those universities. That way lies reputation, prestige and satisfaction. Anyone who takes part in school prize-giving ceremonies knows that the announcement of the pupils who have won a place at Oxford or Cambridge is one of the proudest moments in the headmaster's speech and the occasion for the greatest applause from the parents. The school has arrived. It does not matter that some of the graduates of those ancient universities may not be able to get a job. It does not matter that some of those undergraduates may be deeply unhappy. It does not matter that some who have just scraped in may find it difficult to cope with the studies as well as the life of the university. What matters is that they have got there. Happiness is assured. The evidence of history is that they will do well in life and start with a lead over everyone else. There will be a good job in the Foreign Office or the administration of the British Empire. And if the Foreign Office is not particularly significant nowadays and takes on fewer people, and if the British Empire has been dissolved and there are no large posts for the graduates at all, what does that matter? They will be well turned out, articulate, able to hold their own in a conversation and take up the position of seniority to which they are entitled. The headmaster can rest content. His job has been satisfactorily completed.

The reason for discussing this in a little detail is not to protest about it, but to make a simple and crucial point

— that this experience, not just of Oxford and Cambridge, but of any university and any polytechnic, the experience, of higher education, belongs to less than one in five of the boys and girls who go through the schools. What is called the age participation rate (that is, the proportion of the school-leaving age group who go on to any form of higher education) is just under 13 per cent. If you add to that figure those who will go on to other kinds of training, such as army officers' schools and some private colleges, it is still under 20 per cent. So less than one in five will go on to higher education. Yet the entire school curriculum is aimed at this minority. (It may be the vast majority in the best public schools; but it is not even a majority in some of the less efficient independent schools; it is far from a majority in the state system, not because it is inherently less efficient but because by definition it is comprehensive, catering for boys and girls of all abilities and backgrounds.) What a system of schooling that is geared to less than one in five of the children who experience it!

I am assuming that the education of the vast majority of the boys and girls in this country is, and will in the foreseeable future remain, comprehensive — that is, covering all abilities and interests. I have called that a comprehensive *system*. I am by no means convinced that the only way to organize a comprehensive system is to restrict the provision to comprehensive schools. The belief that all schools should be comprehensive is a political view, and like a lot of political platforms it is simpler to believe that and simpler to organize. There is nothing like a simple general statement for enabling you to avoid coping with the intricacies of a problem.

There is no alternative to a comprehensive *system*, because that is what the state is obliged by the Education Acts from 1870 onwards to provide, and also obliged by its moral responsibility to provide for all. But that does not mean that all schools should be the same in constitution. It may be that we need many different kinds of school, especially for those who approach the senior classes. Within the present system the majority of children have taken crucial decisions (or had crucial decisions taken for them) by the age of 14. After that the school curriculum narrows down their choices. But that must suit a minority only. The vast majority of children have little idea at that age what they are likely or want to do in life. It would in every way be to the good if those decisions could be postponed, as the French do for their high-standard baccalauréat. The Americans too retain a broader subject base right up to high school, sometimes insisting on a practical subject at sixth form level. (The academics can choose typing and later make a living while they research, typing other people's theses.)

But however much these decisions are postponed it must be the case that, by the time they are 16, pupils will have begun to select their studies and discover their interests. It would be good though for pupils to postpone their detailed choices and keep their options as wide open as possible for as long as possible.

The part that we should not exclude as early as we usually do is that part of the mind and of experience which cater for action as well as for book learning. Whitehead makes the point in relation to a technical education:

> we must rise above the exclusive association of learning with book-learning ... The peculiar merit of a scientific education should be, that it bases thought upon first-hand observation; and the corresponding merit of a technical education is, that it follows our deep natural instinct to translate thought into manual skill, and manual activity into thought.

Let me go back to the public schools again, or at least to

the boarding schools. It has for long been recognized that the activities outside the classroom in such schools are an integral part of the education they offer. The school is not, afer all, concerned only with training the mind; there are other important aspects including physical development and health and other community activities — discussion and debates, singing and playing music, painting and drawing, plays and games. Waterloo was won on the playing fields of Eton not just because its former pupils were fit (if indeed they were) but because what the playing fields had taught them was teamwork. However selfish some games may seem to be, it is not easy to win team games without some team spirit and cooperation. What the playing fields offer is not only leisure and recreation, it is a crucial part of the education.

The problem lies with the competitive-minded state school in which that part of the total education can easily be neglected in pursuit of academic results. There are also problems for the teachers; it is easier for a residential master in a boarding school to take an active part in games than for a teacher in a day school for whom games are an added chore unlikely to contribute to promotion.

The moment you see all the activities of a school as making up the meaning of the whole and being essential to the educational experience it changes your idea of the balance of educational endeavour. It should not change your perception of the needs of individual children. Some cannot play games without misery; some must play games and are unhappy about them. All require activity of some kind. The case for Capability in the schools has to do with that. If the balance is wrong and more weight should be given to the culture of doing, making and organizing then it is essential that that should start in school. The irony is that it does so. It starts in the primary school, if not already in the family, and involves the whole person, in learning and play, in creative activity of many kinds and many kinds of expression – drawing and painting, music and singing. The role of play is essential. It is in the secondary school, with its obsession with examinations, that the pattern becomes distorted. It is also in the secondary school that a lot of the disaffections of the teenager are born. *Education is no longer a total experience but a forcing of part of the mind.* In fact, what is relevant is not only the mind but the emotions and the affections, actions and the will.

Let me dwell for a moment on play. Play, as some of the most eminent psychiatrists and philosophers have said, is part of the creative personality of man. It may even be an essential component of art, or at least makes possible an understanding of art in a wider way than usual. It involves both sides of the mind, action as well as thought, determination and persistence, self-control, clarity of mind, and the concentration of excluding other things while pursuing it as an occupation for a limited period of time. It also plays a crucial part in psychological and character growth through the exercise of the imagination. In that sense play is an essential part of the educational experience. There is also another dimension to it which is unpopular with certain politicians but is surely essential to the reaching of any kind of maturity. That is the recognition that whatever you may believe about the classroom, there is no question of equality on the games field. It is surely one of the most valuable experiences for any boy or girl to recognize that people have different abilities, are stronger or weaker, more or less healthy, quicker or slower. There is no evidence whatever that the most brilliant in the classroom are the most clumsy in the field or that the most brilliant player is a dunce in school; often the opposite. The myth of equality which bedevils all sorts of educational theorizing cannot be sustained in the light of sport. *Capability is concerned with the whole person* and any educational theory built upon it must emphasize the whole person and the abilities of widely different kinds that have to be developed and known. It therefore follows that any reform of schooling must involve all sorts of activity as well as book learning — speaking, acting, playing games, playing music, singing. You cannot sing successfully in a choir unless you learn to listen to other people rather than yourself.

To take the matter further, can we decide if there are certain general skills as well as specific ones that everyone ought to learn or develop in themselves and which will be adaptable so as to be applicable in the new situation. We live, after all, in a world which is changing rapidly; we ought, think some theorists, to be re-trained for new jobs three or four times in our lifetime. It used to be thought that there were certain subjects that would be useful no matter what you did in life; is the same true of skills? I have no doubt that it is. Let me take a few, ranging from intellectual habits to more manual ones.

It cannot be a bad thing to learn to concentrate on a problem to the exclusion of everything else for a limited period of time, to exclude distractions and concentrate the mind and the body. It is a myth promoted by the idle that you concentrate better with a lot of noise around, such as perpetual *muzak*. *It cannot be a bad thing to learn to observe external things accurately*, to look hard and note characteristics, to learn the habit of working out what it looks like on the other side and working out how it is built or works, whether it is a snail or a bird or a machine. Observation is sharpened by knowledge. It cannot be a bad thing to learn to concentrate on certain sounds and distinguish them, if only for your own safety. *It cannot be a bad thing to learn how to work a simple machine*, to understand how it works and know when it is going wrong. It cannot be a bad thing to learn how to steer or control a machine, whether a car or a static machine. *Finally, it cannot be a bad thing to learn how to manipulate tools*, to synchronize hand and eye, to manipulate physical objects. Today we would add keyboard skills, an area in which the young learn very quickly, whether for computers or for electronic keyboards.

To take the matter further would require more experience that I have of schools. But in 1977 a group of Her Majesty's Inspectors of Schools produced a report and working papers on the subject *Curriculum 11–16*, which reflects some hard and constructive thinking. In pursuit of a common curriculum they listed areas of experience as a checklist for the curriculum – the aesthetic and creative, the ethical, the linguistic, the mathematical, the physical, the scientific, the social and political, and the spiritual. They gave an interesting and provocative list of the skills in which all school-leavers should be competent.

There would be wide agreement that most pupils should:

    (i)   be able to participate effectively in a conversation; set down clearly what they want to express; write letters and simple descriptive reports

    (ii)   be at ease with diagrams, symbols and graphs; have competence in arithmetic; understand money and the common units of measurement; use a pocket calculator

    (iii) possess the dexterity and physical control necessary to develop manipulative skills

    (iv) be able to draw on and apply the skills required to tackle a problem scientifically

    (v)   have developed capacity for reasoning and judgement.

I tried that out as soon as I read it on some of my own

children and one instantly commented that while the list
was generally excellent it was entirely self-centred and left
out:

(vi)   be able to get on with other people
(vii) work and play in a team.

It seems clear to me that even though some, though not
many, of those items can be learned by rote or discussion,
the vast majority can only be learned by practice. In fact,
not one of those skills can be learned passively or through
simple instruction. You cannot learn to do a single one without
actually doing it, not even developing a capacity for reasoning
and judgement. I do not know of any way to learn the
skill of judgement except by judging things. Games are very
good for it: billiards are excellent practice; so is organizing
a cricket field; so, superlatively, is producing a play, taking
part in a debate or organizing a meal. I have heard it argued
that all those skills are contained in the work of institutional
management or home economics, for men as well as women.
Organizing an exhibition, a demonstration or a publicity
campaign, producing a magazine or a tape or film programme,
writing a computer program — all these are activities which
call for the exercise of judgement in setting up, editing and
scrapping ideas and work. They are also areas of team work,
areas in which modern technology can play a major part.

Let me take the argument a final step. If my argument
is right, it follows that a great deal of education — more
than at present — must proceed by way of projects, set tasks
that at different levels of experience will test students out
and enable them to discover for themselves. And which have
other valuable characteristics. For example, a good project
has to be finished in order to be any good at all. It may
also go wrong several times, and those are crucial lessons

for the real world – how to deal with things without all the information, how to finish a job or discover that it cannot be done, how to cope when things go wrong. On a practical note, project teaching does demand smaller class sizes. Otherwise it is always the same pupils (the natural leaders) who shoulder the responsibility and gain the learning experience.

It is not part of my intention to outline a curriculum. That will come with a National Curriculum. In any case it is not the purpose of this book to specify in detail; what I am concerned with is an attitude. It would require detailed work by people in the field to present a daily timetable for an Education for Capability. In any case I am not at all convinced that curricula should be worked out in too much detail. There is a lot to be said – and it is one of the lessons of the better public schools – for the best teachers being given freedom to devise the curricula for their pupils, matching their needs with the demands and ultimately the needs of society.

What I am concerned about is a matter of principle. It follows from everything I have written above that secondary schooling requires a drastic review, by teachers, of the process whereby they teach most subjects. There may be some subjects that are best taught by the discursive method of starting by teaching generalizations and then working towards applications and examples. There cannot be many. I am convinced that for most people the most efficient way to learn is from experience, from the knowledge of the known to the discovery of the unknown, from the ability to do a simple thing to the discovery of how to do complex things. The way to coordinate all the powers of mind and will and body is to study with all of them; and that means working from the simple and the small-scale to the more complex and large-scale . There is no substitute for the direct perception of the concrete achievement of a thing in its actuality.

11 After School

In any attempt to make changes and improvements in the world of education, *the biggest barrier to improvement is the existence of institutions*. That is probably true for many episodes in history. If nothing else, a high proportion of any institution's time and money is spent keeping itself in existence even if it does nothing. All this was forcibly pointed out by the radical educationist Ivan Illich in *Deschooling Society*. Institutions are by nature conservative. Why should there be radical change if the institution is the repository of inherited ways of doing things and is expected to hand on its traditions? Any proposals for change are likely to be met with anxiety and the closing of ranks against an enemy. The resistance of the multifarious engineering institutions to the proposals for giving the profession a new lease of life in the Finniston Report is typical. Change might be for the worse.

But change is necessary in the educational world. Not radical and destructive change, such as Illich suggested, but – as the Capability manifesto insisted – a change in the balance of education. Even so it will be resisted; and it will be resisted as much as anywhere in the universities. 'The universities', in Whiteheads words,

> are schools of education, and schools of research. But the primary reason for their existence is not to be found either in the mere knowledge conveyed to the students or in the mere opportunities

for research afforded to the members of the faculty.... The justification for a university is that it preserves the connection between knowledge and the zest of life, by uniting the young and the old in the imaginative consideration of learning.

It might be thought that the universities would be at the very centre of discussion and experiment in education; it is one of their functions to act as a critical centre, to examine problems without self-interest, to pursue arguments wherever they may lead irrespective of the consequences, to engage in the dispassionate search for truth. Yet the strange truth is that many universities are resistant to any kind of change. Why should this be? There is no one reason, but a collection of motives, both rational and irrational. It may be thought in some universities that any change can only be a change for the worse. After 700 years of growth it is unlikely that anything worth while has not already been thought of. It may be that the cause of rigidity is simply idleness. There is nothing an academic likes more than sitting for ever on university committees. But there is more to it than that. What is most powerful in the end is the university ethos.

It is difficult to isolate the source of that ethos. But anyone who has worked for more than a year or two in a university will know it. It seems to be a combination of leisure, remoteness from day-to-day pressures, opportunity to think and discuss at length, articulateness and the ability to play with words, the adoption of a civilized way of life, and the formation, however indirectly and however coloured by malice and spite, of a community. You may not know exactly what it is but recognize it when you are there. You may not be able to specify a good academic but you can spot him or her as soon as you start talking, and maybe just from the way he or she walks across the square.

The fact is that the academic way of life is a good one. There is nothing to compare with it. Where else can you find a job at a relatively early age, say in your twenties after study in a fine environment, which gave you security for the rest of your life, whether or not you do any worthwhile work and whether or not you can teach or even want to, with a salary which increases with inflation, promotion to a reasonable level, and a guaranteed index-linked pension at retirement? There are extended vacations, for the sake of doing research and study, and travelling in pursuit of knowledge, there are easy hours, all sort of perquisites, all sorts of rewards, and nothing to prevent you from doing other work at the same time for money and running your own business for profit. And on top of it all, if you become a professor, there is a title which will in Britain, and in most other countries, award instant prestige and status and guarantee a reasonable level of respect and deference from the common man. Despite all that, or perhaps because it seems so improbable that there must be a weakness some- where, academics are as psychologically insecure as anyone else and paranoid about attacks by outsiders. Even though they are supported from the public purse and receive their money indirectly from the taxpayer, they become angry at any suggestion that the public might have views on what they do.

The adoption of the university ethos was nowhere more clearly revealed than in what happened to the Colleges of Advanced Technology (CATs) when, following a recommend- ation in the Robbins Report, they were designated as universities. They were to become technological universities and were expected to concentrate on that important field of work; but within a few years all except one had dropped 'technology' from their title and all had set up courses that would bring them into line with the other universities pursuing the liberal arts, the humanities and often the remoter aspects of them. What that reflected was the inevitable pressure in any university, not to stop the useful subjects but to esteem more highly the cultural subjects and to treat learning as being for its own sake. But the essence of the university ethos is not in what it teaches but in the way it does it. In that sense it is also now (though it was not always so) a central belief that teaching is not the real business of the university teacher (even though that is what he is paid to do); the real business of a university teacher is to do research. It is a consoling thought that the results of any research, no matter how trivial, will be of value to society and give due recognition and status to the researcher.

It has already been described how the development of higher education in Britain contrasted with that in Europe in the nineteenth and twentieth centuries. For this reason it was a major and unexpected change when one drastic innovation was made by the government in the mid-1960s, between Anthony Crosland's Woolwich speech of 1965, the White Paper of 1966 and the designation of new institutions in 1969 and 1970. That was the establishment of the new polytechnics.

Although conventional academics did not notice it at the time, nothing could have had a more fundamental effect on the higher education scene. For one thing, *it introduced a new name*. Education after school was no longer just universities and a bewildering constellation of other colleges that the universities did not know existed. Now it was 'higher education', a wider concept. And within a year of the establishment of the polytechnics it became impossible to speak only of universities; it was necessary to speak of universities *and* polytechnics. The advantage of the wider term 'higher education' is that it also incorporates the many colleges which teach advanced level studies, including degrees. At one stroke the scope of higher education was not only wider but *seen to be wider*. Degrees were no longer rewards for learning for its own sake and the start of another life, finding a job and learning one; degrees were now being precisely planned for vocations. *The measure of a polytechnic's serious work was that it trained for vocations.* The creation of the polytechnics can thus be seen as higher education's contribution to a comprehensive system of education in the UK. It followed that polytechnics themselves must be comprehensive. If they were concerned with vocational training, their scope must encompass all sorts of occupations, in industry and commerce, in the service industries, in health and social work, in the creative arts and in teaching. And that was logical because of their origins. The new polytechnics were in the main formed by the amalgamation of Colleges of Technology, Commerce, Art and Education.

Leeds will serve as an example, partly because I know it at first hand and played a major part in its formation and subsequent enlargement, and partly because it is typical of many of the larger polytechnics in its composition and its problems. What may not be so typical of them in practice, though it is typical in theory, is that Leeds has followed the path set for the polytechnics in the 1966 White Paper and concentrated on vocational education, the maintenance and expansion of part-time courses and the retention of courses below degree level that form a natural part of the corpus of a polytechnic's work and enable students to move in either direction. Some of these are well below degree level; a major group — and this is an important aspect of a polytechnic's character — are the courses leading to what used to be Higher National Diplomas and Higher National Certificates and have now become qualifications validated by the Business and Technician Education Council. Furthermore, wherever possible, courses are sandwich courses, with varying periods in industry or the professions or social services alternating with academic studies in the polytechnic.

That has a significant bearing upon developments and innovation. *It has been a policy in looking at any proposed new course that there should — at least in principle — be a job at the end.* The problems created by the present recession are not peculiar to Leeds; the difficulty in obtaining jobs or placements for training does not require changing a policy which will be appropriate in better economic circumstances.

Nor is Leeds in any way unique in insisting on the importance of sandwich courses. Some of the most insistent protagonists of that system have been the former Colleges of Advanced Technology, for example Bradford and especially Brunel University, where all courses are sandwich courses and where all the evidence is that the courses are the better for it, that the students get jobs and that the link between the university and industries has led to joint exercises in research and development work, enriching both the university and the industries associated with it.

The problems faced by the polytechnics are easy to see and very difficult to resolve. First of all, *they will not succeed if they do not achieve some kind of status in this status-ridden country.* Canon George Tolley, the first Principal of Sheffield Polytechnic, spoke from experience and conviction at the Royal Society of the Arts in April 1986. The title of his paper was *Putting labels on people: the qualifications business,* and in this paragraph he talks about the status problem:

It is one of the ironies of our culture and tradition and of our language, that an 'academic' qualification (which one might think would relate to theoretical and scholarly attributes, eschewing practical application) is the label that exerts the major conditioning influence upon our education system, carrying with it an esteem built upon lack of understanding, misconception and, some might think, magic. The esteem, or lack of it, afforded to a 'vocational' qualification all too often reflects the striking polarity between the words 'vocation' and 'vocational'. It is one of the paradoxes of our vocabulary that 'vocation', whilst not a well-used word, is a high-sounding word of quality, whereas 'vocational' has about it the air of second rate. 'Vocation' conjures up a vision of a calling, a dedication, that is wholly admirable. 'Vocational' has come to mean preparation for a trade or occupation; it tells of narrowness, or restriction, of training for some end that has little to do with the high calling of a vocation. A great deal of our history and of the reasons for our economic decline is encapsulated in that paradox of meaning.

The effects of this paradox were all too easily seen when the polytechnics were set up in the early 1970s. At that time the majority of the students were university failures (That has changed dramatically in the last 15 years. My impression now is that over 60 per cent of polytechnic students are first-choice polytechnic; in some areas, of course, 100 per cent.) Some felt so rejected, having been told by their teachers and parents that they were failures, that it could take six months to persuade them that all was not lost after all. It is one of the commonest experiences of polytechnic teachers to learn from students that whereas they came in despair, after a few months they wouldn't change to another institution for anything. It is so common a story it is not possible to quantify it. If nothing else, there is much to be said for being successful in what you do and finding that you are good at what you do rather than mediocre at what you should never have tried.

Secondly, there is the problem of the staff. Rather like the students, some have been conditioned by their own student days and by popular opinion to believe that they must become as like university teachers as possible. If only they can show that they are useless, they will be recognized as estimable people and in due course receive public awards. Rather as in the case of students, that has changed. There are now, after a decade of development, many polytechnic teachers who are proud of what they do and would not change if they had the choice. The focus of that problem now is the question of professors. Most polytechnics have decided that they must have professorships, not as a title given to the head of department like a university chair, but a title of honour given to an individual, like a personal professorship in a university. It is a controversial matter. The arguments in favour are that only thus will recognition be given to polytechnics as being respectable institutions and that only thus will the polytechnics be able to attract research and other funds. There is nothing like the name professor for influencing an industrialist to part with his money. And the thought of endowing a chair, even in a polytechnic, is thought by some to be one of the great boons brought by them upon mankind. Finally, there is nothing like the pride of a teacher upon being designated professor. Some change their personalities overnight; the road to Damascus is lined with professorial chairs. And even if they themselves don't change, the attitude of everyone else does. An instant opinion by a professor is given more respect than months of thought by a lecturer.

The disadvantages are partly contained in those remarks but more in the obvious implication that such a polytechnic is trying to be as like a university as possible, moving from the service to the autonomous tradition. How soon, it is asked, will they want to drop their part-time work, shed the sub-degree courses, engage only in research to the neglect of their students, and develop a university ethos removed from the urgent practicalities of day to day?

Thirdly, there is the problem of the courses. Should they remain as practical and vocational as possible, or should they become more like university courses? Should they be organized on subject or discipline lines or be course-based and vocational? Should they follow conventional processes, starting with the teaching of generalities and abstractions in the first year — basic courses in maths and physics, and so on — and before the end of the three years looking at applications and real problems; or should they start with the real, the particular, the known, and work towards the formulation of general rules. *I believe a polytechnic study should be conducted in such a way as to teach a skill or skills so well and so fundamentally that it becomes possible for the student to extract from the experience a general principle that will then be applicable in a situation unforeseen.* The problem with that is not just persuading the academic staff to consider it. Some, because of their own training, will never be able to think of a course in any but conventional terms. Others have obtained experience in other institutions and other countries and have begun to question the inevitability of the traditional method, calculated to create the maximum boredom and keeping the attention away as long as possible from real issues. The problem is that there are profound pressures upon the polytechnics to avoid experiment and stick to known respectable methods. Judith Judd, interviewing Christopher Ball, Chairman of the National Advisory Body (which advises the government on higher education outside the universities) for an *Observer* article in 1986, reports him thus:

Academic drift remains a problem, Ball says. All universities try to be like Oxford and Cambridge and all polytechnics like universities.... 'We live in a deeply snobbish society,' says Ball, 'and employers are as snobbish as anybody.' If some polytechnics have concentrated too rigidly on single honours degree courses it is because of pressure from parents and employers.

There are two sources of such pressure, other than the

natural caution of the academic mind and the snobbishness of which Ball was speaking. One was the indirect effect of the amalgamation with the teacher training colleges, either from the beginning or from the cutting back of the colleges in the late 1970s and the replacement of some of the teacher training courses with other diversified courses. The problem was that only a proportion of the academic staff in the colleges were capable of teaching on other polytechnic courses; and very few of them were of sufficient standard to move to a university, to the kind of study which they had believed it right to emulate at a lower level. To that problem there is no solution other than time. However many active teachers have changed direction, gone on courses and acquired new skills, there remains an irreducible minimum who cannot do anything else but what they were trained to do. More far-reaching is the influence of the Council for National Academic Awards. The CNAA was set up at the time of the great expansion of higher education to validate national degrees and diplomas for the polytechnics and the colleges which offer advanced courses. Its influence on academic standards has been positive. It does not lay down what an institution should do but examines proposals initiated and submitted by the institution and either validates them for a fixed or indefinite period or engages in detailed discussions leading to modifications and improvements. It has the great advantage of setting standards which the institution itself might not be able to insist upon, forcing it to examine itself critically and putting pressure upon the authority to provide better resources. It is frequently recognized by university staff taking part in the exercise that the CNAA demands higher standards of provision and preparation of courses than their own universities demand for their own degrees.

That indicates both the strength and the danger of the CNAA. The professional academic staff taking part in its work do so for nothing and work very hard. The polytechnic staff, from many polytechnics, can be even more rigorous in their demands than the university members. The danger is that they may insist upon a university-type course, upon structuring the studies in a way that they are familiar with and urging the institution to adopt the university ethos.

But the greatest problem besetting the polytechnics has been their relationship with the local authorities that own them. It is not always recognised that at the time of writing polytechnics are owned by the local authorities; they do not have corporate status, they have no bank account, they are dependent upon the local authority for their money and the permission to carry out their day-to-day activities. Furthermore, a common policy of local authorities is to subordinate the polytechnic to two different committees — the education committee for courses and academic staff and another committee (often the establishment committee) for non-academic staff, technicians, administrators, secretarial and service staff. Nothing could be more confusing or wasteful of time and energy. It has the advantage to the local authority of keeping the polytechnic in confusion and therefore under control; it has the disadvantage that it makes coherent planning impossible and destroys any sense of unity.

The point I am getting round to is that *the future of the polytechnics is bound up with the need to take them away from the local authorities*. The link seemed sensible when they were set up. After all, the polytechnics were part of a comprehensive provision of higher education, involving part-time and full-time, sub-degree and degree; where better should they be than with the local authorities responsible for the schools and for the further education establishments whose work overlaps with them? It seemed logical in principle; it has proved unworkable in practice. *Local authorities are geared to local needs; the polytechnics are there to satisfy national demands.*

There is no way in which the satisfaction of local concerns can avoid the frustration of national needs. The ultimate irresponsibility of local government is to fail in its national task because of its obsession with local pride and local issues.

It seems obvious to me that the scene of education after school is never likely to be tidy. Institutions do not confine themselves within theoretical boundaries and behave in only one way. Some of the polytechnics are more like universities. Some of the universities are rapidly developing polytechnic-type courses and looking more keenly at vocational needs especially at a time of lack of money. I believe there should be much more variety between institutions, not less, more experiment in their courses rather than standardization, more flexibility in their staff conditions than the conventional tenure for life, more links with the world at work.

I have reviewed some of the main spheres of activity and tried to establish where they are different from one another. But the most intractable problem besetting the scene in this country is the fate of the 16–19 age group. It is a problem that focuses many of the issues which this book has been about and may provide a clue to the way changes might be made.

The problem of the 16–19 age group reflects the problem of education as a whole because as soon as one posits the possibility and the necessity of education for all it raises the question at what age education should be terminated. It is easy to say in comfort that education is life-long or 'permanent', and to advocate the value of continuing education. The notion of continuing education is attractive because it puts off the decision about what should be taught here and now; it is popular with academics because it combines an impression of the maximum of detached wisdom with the minimum of actual commitment. But for the majority of people that is merely a formula. For the majority of boys and girls education of any formal kind stops at the age of 16. A minority will go on to higher education; more will go to some form of further education; the great majority, about four out of five, are expected to go straight into some kind of employment. The employment prospects are at present dauntingly bad, and although they may improve if and when the recession comes to an end, things will never be quite the same again; modern technology must reduce the need for certain kinds of job — at one time the repetitive manual jobs created by the Industrial Revolution, now increasingly the repetitive jobs in the service sector, like typing and paperwork of many kinds. The very jobs which were most readily available to the school-leavers look like being the very jobs which are most likely to disappear.

Secondly, the prospects will continue to look less good because of the absolute decline in the number of apprenticeships available, the openings which enable a school-leaver to go straight to work and get on-the-job training, supplementing it when necessary by attendance at evening or part-time day classes. It is a matter of the utmost significance for the future of the country. *The key to the disappearance of apprenticeships*, in marked contrast to some other countries, *is not only the unwillingness of employers to take on unskilled labour; it is the policy of the unions, confirmed by the Trade Union Council, that the hallowed system of collective bargaining means that apprentices must come within the terms of that bargaining and must therefore be paid almost the same as skilled experienced workers.* That arises from the suspicion of the trade unions that low-paid apprentices would otherwise get jobs which ought to be filled by experienced workers. It is the most shortsighted and destructive policy. No sensible employer will, except for idealistic reasons, take on an apprentice when for only a little more money he can get an experienced man; in the long term it is robbing the country of skills, and individuals of the satisfaction of learning skills and finding their identity in work.

Given that problem, it is difficult to see any immediate solution and it is therefore necessary to work towards another solution on the assumption that the number of apprenticeships will not be increased. Young people without work must at least be taught the skills which they would otherwise have acquired at work and be able in due course to take their place as skilled workers. But if everything I have written so far is valid, the only way to acquire such skills must be by doing and making rather than by being told about it, and therefore training in action is essential to the solution of the problem.

The characteristic changes in technology mean that work alone will not be enough; nor some minor supplementation with evening classes. What is needed is an education and training in thinking and action that draws upon both employment or work and instruction in colleges, integrated into a meaningful learning experience. If it is to be genuinely unified it will not do to lay on a few lectures; the learning part in the classroom must be as much workshop as classroom, capable of bridging between work on the shopfloor and the acquisition of general rules. That requires teachers who know the work at first hand and how to interpret it. And not only to interpret it: to see also how it may change and equip the student/apprentices with an understanding of work in the midst of change. The machinery of political change works slowly. We may be beginning to see that challenge taken up by extended Manpower Services Commission schemes, and government plans for new inner-city crown colleges.

The type of programme where the week is divided into several days at work under the supervision of an experienced foreman and several days in college with a mixture of classes and workshops, building on the experience of the shopfloor and seeing its relevance to the learning of the classroom, has long been in force in Industrial Language Training units for those entering our workforce for whom English is a second language. The system appears to work well, with the two types of learning complementing each other. Why should these methods not be available to the general public? Obviously, such schemes need to be well funded. But *in what way is it fair that grants should be available to those who have done well at school and go on to higher education, but not to those whose skills at work would benefit the whole country?*

The need is recognized by all political parties and the machinery is there. The Youth Opportunities Programme brought it to notice; the Manpower Services Commission has the resources, the energy and the capacity to promote schemes. Now we have the proposed technical colleges, still largely at discussion stage as this book goes to print, and at the moment only planned for a small number of inner-city areas. While work remains the key to identity, to pride and self-respect and to independence, work opportunities have to be created. We need a new approach to apprenticeship and a full use of the programmes already launched. The work may have to be simulated but it is essential that it should have the reality of discipline and an adult atmosphere.

Nor is there any reason to think it cannot be done. John Tomlinson, formerly Director of Education for Cheshire and Chairman of the Schools Council, pointed out in a paper of 1981 *On Looking at the 80'(s)*:

when the Youth Opportunities Programme began to tackle the problem of how to make these youngsters employable an interesting discovery was made: they were educable. More-

over it was found that what they lacked first and foremost
was self-confidence and the basic skills of social competence,
for coping with the complexities of everyday life. Given a
chance to gain some self-confidence, the other basic skills
of numeracy and literacy, which had often eluded them for
11 years of schooling, also came within their grasp.

His comments are in line with the findings of the originators
and teachers on the Adult Literacy Campaign, where great
pains are taken not to reproduce the situation and atmosphere
which for these students smacks of failure, and to teach the
skills through material (that is, directly and perceptibly)
relevant to the students' life needs. (Reading and numeracy
are, after all, only tools: they are not ends in themselves.)

John Tomlinson advocated a more balanced form of secondary education, which would ensure that as many pupils as
possible gained the self-confidence which arises from finding
that you can do something reasonably well. We have committed the folly of creating a failure group (worse, a *majority*
failure group) and then have had to spend money to put
it right, with massive transfers of non-DES money to compen-
sate for the failure of educational policy and practice.

I commented above that the issue of the 16–19 age group
focuses the problems of education and society, of education
for today. In that context no two factors are more important
than, on the one hand, the belief that there should be education
for all, and, on the other hand, the recognition that the
pattern of work is changing and will not provide jobs for
the people who cannot, or do not want to, pursue education
for the rest of their lives. The conclusion from those two
factors is not that we should retreat into an educational system
of passive instruction, of inert knowledge and criticism, so
that everyone with an education will be fitted to watch
television for the rest of their lives if they do not have

a job. The conclusion is that in an increasingly do-it-yourself society we need skills in any case. Everyone, no matter how clever or unclever, will need skills of some sort. In the event of further technological change and expansion people will need skills of a higher sort, preferably transferable skills. In the more advanced reaches of work and discovery in an advanced modern society, very high-level skills will be needed, not just for the also-rans, but for the very brightest. If we can find a solution to the problem of the 16–19 year olds we have the clues to the rest.

Postscript: Competence and Freedom

In the daily grind of devising and running courses of instruction, discussing day-to-day affairs, and recruiting and examining students, it is easy to find that the last thing ever to be discussed is the ultimate question: *What is it that we are educating and training our pupils and students for?* Ironically, there is no shortage of political agitation and propaganda in the universities and colleges. A large number of academic staff see political activity as central to their work and courses, as well as to their research. Many seem to look forward to a totalitarian political system in which, presumably, they themselves will have the power; the possibility – indeed, the certainty – of intellectual submission and conformity does not deter or in any way dismay the protagonists of the totalitarian state. I think it is therefore important to review the basic beliefs that underlie the policies developed in this book, especially because the use of modern technology can be an effective vehicle for slavery and control. Because most of my arguments centre upon exploiting to the full the use of modern technology, it is incumbent upon me to clarify what I believe in socially and politically, and then see if that is compatible with the fuller use of technology and design.

Any educational programme would, I feel, be dangerous if it did not accept as fundamental the recognition of the existence, and the need to increase, man's freedom. Freedom must be the ultimate aim and safeguard of any system. *Any policy that limits man's freedom must belong to an alien political view;* anyone therefore who believes in imposed equality and compulsory regulation of the lives of the people will have no sympathy for this study. There are plenty of protagonists of slavery and they can be found and consulted.

For many people the attraction of such a system is its certainty. If everything is regulated and made compulsory a great weight of responsibility is lifted off the shoulders; the state will let you know what to think, so all you have to do is concentrate on your work and keep in line. The state will of course also be inefficient and clumsy in setting up its programmes; being itself composed of a mass of people agreeing a policy, it is unlikely that much will be done or changed in a hurry. The bureaucracy of mass control is internationally known; it creates lots of jobs, which makes it popular with a certain kind of person and shares out the responsibility so that no one individual has to feel responsible or guilty. The decision is taken by the group and every member of it can insist on his or her independence from the collective view.

It is central to my thinking that the mark of an educated person is that issues are no longer simple, that they are not black or white, that the truth lies somewhere in the middle and that there is no escape from the responsibility of knowing one's own mind and making one's own decisions. George Scott-Moncrieff, the Scottish writer, once remarked that maturity comes when you cease to blame other people for your own condition. If that is valid it means that *any educational system that fails to make people responsible for themselves must be a failure*. It also follows that such responsibility is a condition for personal freedom.

Freedom is not alway attractive. It requires independence

and the readiness to make judgements as well as to accept responsibility. It makes life more difficult, not less, but also more exciting. There is nothing to compare to the deadly and deadening joylessness of the totalitarian state.

But what is freedom? Freedom is not anarchy; liberty is not licence. *The condition for freedom is order.* Unless there is control and a system for enforcing it, there is no guarantee of people's freedom from the posessiveness and rapaciousness of others. *Laws exist to protect people's freedoms.*

We cannot have freedom without order. Without order there is anarchy or confusion and that leads naturally to tyranny. But there is another special dimension to the problem as it affects us today and that has to do with the complexity of a technological society. *You cannot be free if you do not have some control over your environment.* One of the definitions of technology I used earlier in this book was that it is the process that enables man to control his environment. In that sense the understanding and use of technology is one of the conditions for freedom. Or put it another way; in the modern world you cannot be free unless you understand enough about technology to be able to use it and not be controlled by it.

But no one would claim to understand enough about technology to be able to control all of it. We have to be selective if only because of the scope and complexity of technology. But if we select the section which suits us it is necessary to master it. And if you can master one part of it you can argue that it is not impossible to master other parts of it. But, as I argued earlier, the understanding of technology is not simply a matter of appreciation; it requires using it — that is, doing something, not simply reading about other people doing something. The condition for freedom is thus the possession of sufficient competence to handle the available technology. That means not only that you can control some things and work upon them; it also means that you are able to drive out fear of the man-made world. There is no need to be afraid if you know what is happening and know that you can operate and change things — if you know that you can make and do for yourself, and that you can make and do what you say you can do. *Competence and freedom are interdependent.*

I conclude with two comments. First, competence tells us something about Man's ability to manipulate and work upon things. But what is it in the world of things that you actually know? What you know is not something fixed and finite; that would be artificial knowledge, suitable for examination purposes but remote from the reality of the world. As I suggested earlier in a brief eulogy of the natural world, there is no reason to suppose that we have reached the limits of understanding of that world. There may indeed not be any limits. What we have learned about it suggests that it is a dynamic world, changing its tiniest components. In the world of individual things and of individual artefacts, reality is active and we, the educators and educated, are part of it. The discovery and use of reality involve an active mode of learning.

Secondly, of all the aspects of reality studied, it is lastingly important to discover and understand better the reality and nature of human groups. If our discovery of ourselves is made through the mutuality of relationships and if education is between people and not just an isolated moment, then we ought to know more about human groups —: what size can they be, how do they function, what makes them more or less creative?

There is plenty of evidence of the need for groups to be reasonably small if they are to be creative, responsible and free. As Schumacher wrote in *Small is Beautiful*, we always have a need for both the big-scale and the small-scale; for order and freedom. But it is the smaller group, the understandable group, in which it is possible for each person to know the others and to begin to understand how they will behave, that contains the maximum possibilities for creativity. And also for enjoyment, the enjoyment of being responsible for yourself, having new experiences and making new discoveries.

Index